The SURPASSING GREATNESS OF HIS POWER

RICK JOYNER

 *Whitaker House*

THE SURPASSING GREATNESS OF HIS POWER

Rick Joyner
MorningStar Publications
16000 Lancaster Highway
Charlotte, NC 28277
1-800-542-0278

ISBN: 0-88368-481-0
Printed in the United States of America
Copyright © 1996 by Rick Joyner

Whitaker House
30 Hunt Valley Circle
New Kensington, PA 15068

Library of Congress Cataloging-in-Publication Data

Joyner, Rick, 1949–
    The surpassing greatness of His power / Rick Joyner.
        p.   cm.
    Originally published: [New Kensington, Pa.] : Whitaker House ;
    Charlotte, NC : MorningStar Publications, ©1996.
    ISBN 0-88368-481-0 (trade paper : alk. paper)
    1. Mission of the church. 2. Spiritual warfare. I. Title.
[BV601.8.J69 1997]
269—dc21   97-20962

4 5 6 7 8 9 10 11 12 / 06 05 04 03 02 01 00

Acknowledgements:

Special thanks to the editorial staff for all the hard work and long hours that went into making this book possible: Dianne Thomas, Julie Joyner, Steve Thompson, Becky Chaille, Terri Herrera and Felicia Hemphill.

CONTENTS

Introduction

This is the most extraordinary time ever to be alive. To know the Lord and serve Him in these times is possibly the greatest privilege that has ever been offered to any man or woman, and it has been offered to you. However, with this great privilege comes great responsibility, and with the great opportunities have come great difficulties. In fact, it is probable that it has never been more difficult to be in the ministry. This book was written to help illuminate the honors and responsibilities, the difficulties and the opportunities facing those in ministries today.

Change is now coming upon the world so fast that the only thing we can now count on is change. The foundations of every religion, philosophy and system of government are being shaken. Should we resist change, or help set its course? The answer is both.

If we do not resist the changes that we should resist, we will become subject to changes that we do not want. As the old proverb goes, "The ship in the water is okay, but water in the ship is not!" Much of the church has been sinking under the influence of the humanistic forces she tried to influence when she should have taken a bold stand against them. Very soon the church will be faced with possibly her greatest test in how she relates to the world. Those who do not understand the changes that are coming will be swept away by them. Those who do understand them will be in a position to help direct them. The need for prophetic clarity has never been greater.

Charity With Wisdom

It may be hard to understand now, but one of the greatest attacks coming upon the church will gain entry through her compassion. I must emphasize "her" compassion and not God's compassion. One of the enemy's primary strategies is to wear out the saints. He is doing this by releasing a horde of "false brethren" to steal the children's bread. He will use these false brethren to absorb most of the time, attention and energy of the leadership of the church, so that they will not have anything left for God's people.

These people will be the first in your prayer lines, and try to consume so much of your time and energy that you will not have anything to give to the others. These will crowd around the pastor after every service so that he does not have time to talk with anyone else. They will call you and demand attention at the most inappropriate times, and no amount of attention will ever be enough for them.

These people are not consciously evil, and probably have no idea that they are doing this. Many are just wounded people who need constant affirmation and attention. There is a great danger that once we see this, we will allow ourselves to become hardened to the genuine needs of people. We must walk in discernment or we will constantly be distracted from the ministry God has called us to. Beware of those who are taking most of your time, attention and strength, but are not really changing.

Spiritual Socialism

The above briefly describes Satan's strategy against individual ministers. The following describes a major strategy by which he will seek to entrap the entire church.

The whole world is now beginning to understand that socialism does not work. Socialism conditions people to depend on the government to meet their needs. This can be tolerable at first, but as the people gradually lose their sense of personal responsibility (which inevitably happens under socialism), the government starts to get blamed for every problem, and demands are put upon it to meet every need and want of the people. Soon even hideous crimes are blamed on the social environment, which, of course, is the government's responsibility. It is impossible for any government to sustain these pressures, so it will ultimately collapse.

Possibly the last major institution to understand that socialism will not work is the church. In one sense this is understandable, because we know that God supplies all of our needs. The error is that many have interpreted this as the *church* supplies all of our needs. This delusion will cause the collapse of those who succumb to it. The church is here to help men restore their relationship with God, not take the place of that relationship. The church is not here to meet the needs of the people, but to connect them to the only One who can.

This does not negate acts of charity, which are indeed fundamental to Christianity. However, there is a line that we can easily cross that will actually kill the power of true charity, as well as the church or ministry which crosses it.

Homeless people have recently started coming into our meetings. They are wonderful people, some of whom are really seeking the Lord. Immediately some of our members approached me and asked what the church was going to do for them. "Nothing," was my reply. Because the church as an institution was not going to respond to them, individuals did. True charity must be personal; it must be relational. When we put the responsibility for charity on the institution of the church, we deprive individuals of some of their greatest opportunities to love others. The power of God to meet needs is released through love, not programs.

This is not to imply that there are not some acts of charity that we should do together as a congregation, but we must be careful to only do what we are called to do. Jesus never responded to human need; He only did what He saw the Father doing. We must walk in the same kind of obedience or we will fall into a deadly trap that is set for those who walk in human compassion rather than God's compassion. That trap is a form of socialism that will ultimately separate us from our true Source. It will also wear us out by compelling us to carry the people's yoke instead of the Lord's.

Having said all of this, I know that one of the greatest problems in the church today is not trying to do too much, but not doing enough. We are confronting a great "Laodicean lukewarmness." However, the main reason for this apathy is rooted in the weariness that comes from trying to minister in human compassion rather than by the anointing of the Holy Spirit. The church is worn out from all of the projects and programs forced upon her. The way out of the apathy is not to get the church moving again, but to see her empowered by the presence of the Lord. When she is thus empowered she will see real and lasting fruit from her ministry. She will also walk in the joy of the Lord that is the source of her strength.

An Impending Catastrophe

The Savings & Loan debacle in the U.S. was blamed on crooks and irresponsibility within the industry. These may have contributed to the weakness of the S&Ls, but they were not the reason for the collapse. The collapse was caused by the Reagan Tax Reform Bill. This tax reform was badly needed, and long overdue, but it was implemented in such a way that it devastated commercial real estate values, for which the S&Ls were holding most of the mortgages.

The value of real estate had been wrongly propped up by tax loop holes which needed to be closed. However, changing tax laws in the way that our government has often done it has business caught in something like trying to play a game when the rules are constantly being changed. One minute a move causes you to score, and the next time you move you lose. It is not only frustrating, it prohibits the kind of long term planning that true economic health requires.

If the Reagan Tax Reforms had been phased in over a few years it would have saved us all hundreds of billions of dollars. It was a case of doing the right thing in the wrong way. Now we desperately need to have radical changes made in our welfare system. If we make them too fast the cost will be far more than we will ever save on the budget. As bad as the present rules are, they are the rules that many people have built their lives on.

They will not be able to change their lives as fast as the government will probably require them to. Multitudes of people are about to be devastated. The ultimate losses in both people and property promises to be much greater than we experienced with the S&L collapse. The church and Islam will compete to fill this vacuum. The church is presently not well positioned to engage in one of the greatest battles for the soul of America that has ever been waged.

The Trap Can Be a Door

The church has the power to turn this great impending catastrophe into one of the greatest opportunities for the gospel she has ever had. The enemy's strategy will be to try to get the church to respond to the collapse of socialism with her own form of socialism. This will only result in the church being pulled into the quicksand. If we are going to be able to pull anyone out of the quicksand, we must first be standing on solid ground ourselves. That is the purpose of this book—to return the ministry of the church to solid ground. If she does return, she will be the greatest force for change the world has ever known, and they will be changes that we can all live with.

PART I

The Highest Calling

That He would grant you, according to the riches of His glory, to be strengthened with power through His Spirit in the inner man;

so that Christ may dwell in your hearts through faith; and that you, being rooted and grounded in love,

may be able to comprehend with all the saints what is the breadth and length and height and depth,

and to know the love of Christ which surpasses knowledge, that you may be filled up to all the fulness of God (Ephesians 3:16-19).

CHAPTER ONE

The Majesty Of The Call

If you are a Christian, you are a part of **"a chosen race, a royal priesthood, a holy nation, a people for God's own possession, that you may proclaim the excellencies of Him who has called you out of darkness into His marvelous light" (I Peter 2:9).** There is no greater honor to be found on this earth than to be a minister of Jesus Christ, and *every Christian is called to this ministry.* You are the true nobility. You have a destiny that is so great that the angels in heaven marvel at what God has chosen to do among men.

Even if you were to accumulate all of the power and wealth on the earth it would not measure up to your calling in Christ Jesus. Even the greatest earthly kings have a life that is but a vapor, a wisp of smoke. They all die, and in death their wealth and their exploits are all a part of the dust to which they return. The histories of men will be forgotten; they will pass away with the earth that will one day be rolled up like a scroll. You, on the other hand, will live forever, and your deeds are being recorded in the Book of Life that will never pass away. When measured by the true values of eternity, a day in your life can be more important than the entire reign of earthly kings or presidents. This may seem too fantastic, but it is the word of God, and God cannot lie.

This is not stated to assuage your ego, but to impress upon you the importance of your calling and destiny. Every day in your life has infinite potential and value. You have access to the King of kings. Your petition before Him can change the course of nations.

You not only have access to the King of kings, but you have been sent into this world as His ambassador. To carry God's own words and to convey His purposes is an honor much greater than that of an emissary of any earthly king or president.

Paul's declaration to the Corinthians, that they were **"ambassadors for Christ" (II Corinthians 5:20 KJV)**, was a statement of such power that it probably buckled the knees of those who read it. The assignment of "ambassador" was one of the highest honors that one could receive in the empire. Because communication between a potentate and his ambassador could take months, or even years, those chosen for such a position were the most faithful, loyal friends of the emperor. They had to be of one mind with their leader because they would likely have to make many decisions in his name.

Being an ambassador was one of the greatest honors that a man could be given by his sovereign, but it was also one of great responsibility. A man inclined to speak from his own opinions could never be an ambassador. He had to know the mind of his king, and be utterly faithful to represent only his interests. Because loyalty and faithfulness were so critical, it was the practice of potentates to recall ambassadors after only two or three years of service to a country. They feared that if an emissary stayed away longer he might become too sympathetic with the nation to which he had been sent, and, therefore, be prone to compromise the interests of his homeland.

You are called to be an ambassador of the greatest King. To be an ambassador for Christ is an incomprehensible honor, but it likewise carries the greatest of responsibilities. We must guard our hearts from becoming more sympathetic to the interests of this present age than to the interests of Christ. It was for this reason that Jesus gave Peter possibly the most terrible rebuke recorded in the Scriptures, **"Get behind Me, Satan! You are a stumbling block to Me; for you are not setting your mind on God's interests, but man's" (Matthew 16:23)**. This is still a frequent way that Satan injects his destructive schemes into the church, by causing us to set our minds on man's interests rather than on God's.

As ambassadors of Christ our first devotion must always be to have His perspective. The Lord does not change His ambassadors every two years; we all have a lifetime commission. Therefore, we must be even more vigilant to keep our minds and hearts set on God's interests, alone. As Paul explicitly declared in Galatians 1:10: **"If I were still trying to please men, I would not be a bond-servant of Christ."** When we fear men, seeking the praises or acceptance of men, we will be prone to misrepresent the interests of the kingdom of God.

The Greatest Gift

To perform this great task to which we have been called, the Lord has given us each a gift of power beyond understanding—the Holy Spirit. There is more power resident in the newest believer than there is in all of the armies of the earth combined! The apostle questioned the Corinthians: **"Do you not know that you are a temple of God, and that the Spirit of God dwells in you?" (I Corinthians 3:16).** The Power that created the world lives inside of you! The same Power that performed the greatest miracles in the Bible, stopping the sun, parting seas, or raising the dead, *is in you*. Therefore, you have the potential to do these same works, and according to the Lord Jesus Himself, even "greater works."

As Paul Cain once said, "We are all as close to God as we want to be." This is a biblical truth. **"Draw near to God and He will draw near to you" (James 4:8).** There is no one in the Bible who was closer to God than you can be. Moses talked with God face to face just as a man talks to his friend. He was so close to God that **"the sons of Israel could not look intently at the face of Moses because of the glory of his face" (II Corinthians 3:7).** Moses was so close to God that His glory rubbed off on him. As inconceivable as it seems, you have been called to something even greater. God spoke to Moses face to face, but He has come to live in you!

As awesome as the glory of God on Moses was, Paul continued by saying, **"How shall the ministry of the Spirit fail to be even more with glory?" (verse 8).** By this he was saying that the glory that we are supposed to be experiencing is greater than what Moses experienced, and he had to put a veil over his face because of the glory! When was the last time that you had to wear a veil because the glory of God emanating from your face was scaring people? The only reason why we are not walking in this kind of glory is because we do not want to. We can all be as close to God as we want to be. The ministry of the Spirit is supposed to be **"even more with glory."**

The Scriptures are clear that before the end there will be a church that walks in the glory and purity consistent with her calling. Why not us? Why not now? What do we have to do that is greater than running the race that has been set before us—to be a part of the high calling of God in Christ Jesus? His light will shine upon the earth through the church;

> **Arise, shine; for your light has come, and the glory of the LORD has risen upon you.**
> **For behold, darkness will cover the earth, and deep darkness the peoples; but the LORD will rise upon you, and His glory will appear upon you (Isaiah 60:1-2).**

As this text makes clear, at the very time when darkness is covering the earth, the Lord is going to be so close to His people that His glory will actually appear upon them just like it did Moses. We are coming to those times, but only the most foolish will wait for the darkness to get close to the Lord. King David warned:

> **Therefore, let everyone who is godly pray to Thee in a time when Thou mayest be found; surely in a flood of great waters they shall not reach Him (Psalm 32:6).**

Once the storms have begun, it will be too late to try to rebuild our houses upon the Rock. Once the Bridegroom has called it will be too late to find oil for our lamps. We have been given the greatest of callings, the greatest of opportunities in all of creation. We have been called to be the sons and daughters of the King who is above all kings. To disregard such an honor is to fall to the same tragic fate as Esau, who traded his birthright as an heir of the promises for a mere bowl of soup! How many of us have not traded much more for much less? How many of us have been frivolously wasting our time when we could have spent it before the Throne of Grace? Even so, regardless of the terrible delusions that we have succumbed to, if we repent the Lord can make up all of the ground that we have lost much more quickly than we could ever believe. As Peter explained:

But do not let this one fact escape your notice, beloved, that with the Lord one day is as a thousand years, and a thousand years as one day (II Peter 3:8).

The Lord can do in us in one day what we think would take a thousand years. His grace is not dependent on our abilities or disabilities, or on time. If we repent of walking in the delusions of devotion to things that are temporary, we can right now be as close to Him as we want to be, and our deeds will begin to have the mark of eternity on them—we will begin to bear fruit that remains.

Therefore, let us fear lest, while a promise remains of entering His rest, any one of you should seem to have come short of it.

For indeed we have had good news preached to us, just as they also; but the word they heard did not profit them, because it was not united by faith in those who heard.

For we who have believed enter that rest, just as He has said, "As I swore in My wrath, they shall not enter My rest," although His works were finished from the foundation of the world.

> For He has thus said somewhere concerning the
> seventh day, "And God rested on the seventh day
> from all His works";
>   and again in this passage, "They shall not enter My
> rest."
>   Since therefore it remains for some to enter it, and
> those who formerly had good news preached to them
> failed to enter because of disobedience,
>   He again fixes a certain day, *"Today,"* saying
> through David after so long a time just as has been
> said before, *"Today if you hear His voice, do not harden
> your hearts"* (Hebrews 4:1-7).

In this passage the writer equates the rest of God with the
Promised Land. There is a place of perfect peace, perfect rest,
where we are called to abide. That place is simply the will of
God. King David knew that He could find no rest himself until
the Lord had a permanent place to dwell. We will only find our
rest when we become His dwelling place. Today God is speaking to His people everywhere to return to Him, and to walk
with Him in a manner worthy of our calling. "Today" *you* can
be as close to Him as anyone ever has.

One of the primary characteristics recognized by historians
as a foundation for greatness is *constancy of purpose.* Those who
know their purpose, who set their hearts upon it without
deviating from their course, are the ones who have dictated the
course of history, for good or evil. If you are a Christian then
your potential destiny is greater than that of any conqueror.
What is more important than giving yourself to that destiny?
The purpose of this book is to help you focus on your purpose,
with such a clear, biblical vision that you will be able to maintain
the constancy required for accomplishing all that you were
placed on this earth to do. Paul challenged the church,

> I pray that the eyes of your heart may be enlight-
> ened, so that you may know what is the hope of His

calling, what are the riches of the glory of His inheritance in the saints,

and what is the surpassing greatness of His power toward us who believe. These are in accordance with the working of the strength of His might (Ephesians 1:18-19).

The eyes of our hearts must be opened. If we are walking in reality, what we see with the eyes of our hearts will be more real to us than what we are seeing with our physical eyes. When this happens we will be focused on the **"hope of His calling . . . the riches of the glory of His inheritance"** in us. When that becomes the focus of our vision and purpose, we will begin to walk in the **"surpassing greatness of His power toward us."** That power is greater than any other power in heaven or on earth, and it dwells within you! This is our quest—to walk in the power that has been given to us to manifest the riches of His glory. In the following chapters we will examine the biblical truth and character that is required for this ministry.

CHAPTER TWO

The Crown of Glory

When we consider the power of God we often think of the gifts of the Holy Spirit such as miracles, healing and prophecy. These are great and wonderful gifts, the value of which few of us have even begun to comprehend. However, one of the greatest gifts of all, which has by far accomplished more for the kingdom of God than all of the other gifts combined, is the gift of preaching.

The Glory of Preaching

Jesus is the Word of God. Jesus is the communication of God to His creation. This fact alone elevates the preaching of His word to the highest levels. When the preached word is elevated to the stature which it deserves, it will enable the church to be elevated to the position to which she has been called. If we will give ourselves to understanding the phenomenon of preaching, and devote ourselves to seeing it raised to its rightful position, we will inevitably raise ourselves with it.

The apostle Paul talked about **"the foolishness of preaching"** through which the Lord **"saved those who believe" (I Corinthians 1:21 KJV).** Certainly there is a "foolishness of preaching" when we consider how easy it would be for the Lord to prove Himself by simply writing His name across the sky, or performing some other world-stopping demonstration of His power. But to the spiritual man, preaching is not foolishness, it is a powerful demonstration of the Lord's grace, wisdom and restraint in beckoning His fallen creation to return to Him.

True, anointed preaching is a source of life from beyond this realm that touches us with eternity. Where there is no true preaching there is an obvious absence of resurrection life, and the church will slip back into the tyranny of the temporary and other serious deception. Even when the greatest miracles are worked, preaching is required to explain the demonstrations of God's power and to call men to salvation or repentance.

Like many of the most valuable spiritual words, the very word "preaching" has often been so distorted that it usually arouses images of fists pounding on pulpits, or the ragings of intolerant, angry men. However, let us never forget that this was the primary occupation of most of the righteous men and women who have walked on this earth, including the Lord Jesus Himself. It was also the primary commission which He gave to His disciples, to preach the gospel of His kingdom and to be witnesses of His resurrection.

This has never ceased to be the church's primary calling, and the foundation of all true ministry. We are here first and foremost to *proclaim* the message He has entrusted to us. The ultimate success of our ministry will be determined by how well we proclaim this message. The quality of our message will be determined first by how well we know it ourselves, and then by how well we live it. Therefore, we must have as a primary goal a clear comprehension of the message, and the lifestyle that it demands. It is the goal of this book to weave both of these together.

Only One Yoke

The greatest single contributing factor to spiritual burnout comes from the tendency of those in ministry to take the people's yoke instead of the Lord's yoke. Such a tendency causes not only burnout, but a radical departure from true ministry. In the text from Hebrews 4 quoted in the last chapter, we read how the Lord equated entering His rest with entering the Promised Land. His calling to us remains:

Come to Me, all who are weary and heavy-laden, and I will give you rest.

Take My yoke upon you, and learn from Me, for I am gentle and humble in heart; and you shall find rest for your souls.

For My yoke is easy, and My load is light (Matthew 11:28-30).

To take a yoke speaks of work, but when we are yoked with Him it is His strength that will do the work; we just go along for the ride. When we are yoked with Him, we will find rest for our souls, not weariness. Whenever we become weary, or overly burdened, we have somehow slipped out of His yoke and are carrying our own yoke, or the yokes of others. This is nothing less than to have departed from true ministry. True ministry is an easy yoke. We should find it exhilarating. If this is not the case, we must begin to look for where we missed the turn, because we have departed from His path.

Jesus never responded to human need—He only responded to what He saw the Father doing. He felt compassion for men, but He did not just respond out of compassion; He only responded out of obedience to the Father. Until we have learned to do the same, we will not be entrusted with the same kind of authority and power that He walked in.

The Lord wants us to do even greater works than He did (see John 14:12). This would be one of the greatest evidences that we have come to abide in him. We start by believing *in* the Lord, but His ultimate goal is that we believe *like* Him. It will be in this capacity that He is to be fully manifested in His church. But such authority can only be entrusted to the most loyal, faithful and obedient servants of Christ—not servants of themselves, or of the people.

The failure to keep His interests and perspective foremost is a primary reason for much of the humiliation that has come upon the church in recent years. When a poll was taken ranking the most respected professionals, television preachers were ranked 49th out of 50. Used car salesmen, lawyers and politicians all ranked higher than preachers in the people's trust. This will change, but before it changes, *we* must change.

Those who have been given this greatest of commissions must also live by the highest standards of integrity. The level of integrity that we live by will be determined to a great degree by a single factor: who we live our lives before—the Lord, or the people.

I have had a recurring vision of a pastor that I consider to be one of the most important visions I have ever received. As long as this man keeps his attention focused on the Lord great multitudes gather around him. Every time he takes his attention off of the Lord and looks at the people they start to scatter from him. It is not only apparent that this has happened often in the church, but this could well be the point at which many in ministry make a turn toward an inevitable shipwreck.

Every time those in leadership take their eyes off of the Lord to look at the people, they lose their anointing and the people are scattered. When they look back to the Lord, they will receive the anointing that will draw the people back. That this is a recurring vision speaks to me that it is a recurring problem. Church history testifies that this is indeed the case.

Regardless of how handsome and charismatic we may think we are, if the people are gathering because of us, then we are not building the true church. Paul explained, **"For no man can lay a foundation other than the one which is laid, which is Jesus Christ" (I Corinthians 3:11).** We cannot continue to convert people to our churches, our doctrines, our programs, or our own eloquence as preachers. If people are coming for anything other than the Lord Jesus Himself we are building on a shaky foundation that is doomed to ultimate collapse.

True and False Ministry

The Lord addressed a prevailing problem in the church today through the prophet Jeremiah,

My people have become lost sheep; their shepherds have led them astray. They have made them turn aside on the mountains; they have gone along from mountain to hill and have forgotten their resting place (Jeremiah 50:6).

The people have been led astray by shepherds who try to keep them turning aside, going from mountain to hill, or from one high place to another. This speaks of always trying to keep the people excited and moving, leading them from one project to the next.

By trying to keep the people continually moving and occupied with one project after another, we are depriving them of the very purpose of their calling; to have an intimate, personal relationship with the Lord of the Sabbath, the Lord of rest. One of the fundamental reasons for the pervading Laodicean spirit of lukewarmness in the church is simply because she is worn out because of all of the projects, hype and manipulation.

We are not called to just build ministries, churches, or anything else. The Lord is not building His temple out of organizations and projects—He is building it out of people. The basic issue with every pastor should not be how much his people are doing, but how much of Christ can be seen in them.

From all of our works the only fruit that will truly last is that which has attained Christlikeness. Having organizations or projects is not wrong, but they become idolatry if they displace the Lord as the object of our devotion, and many do. Rare is the organization that has not slipped from building people to "building the ministry."

If we do not keep our attention focused upon the ultimate purpose of God we will continually be deceived by the lesser purposes of God. Deception is not just misunderstanding certain biblical doctrines—deception is not being in God's will. The church has often been distracted from the River of Life by all of the little tributaries which feed it. Good can be the worst enemy of best. The apostle Paul clearly articulated the ultimate purpose of God in Ephesians 1:9-10:

He made known to us the mystery of His will, according to His kind intention which He purposed in Him
with a view to an administration suitable to the fulness of the times, that is, *the summing up of all things in Christ,* things in the heavens and things upon the earth.

Christ Jesus *is* the purpose of God. We can only work to help accomplish His purpose to the degree to which we ourselves have complied with it—through having our own lives summed up in Him. We only have true spiritual authority to the degree to which the King Himself lives within us.

If what we are doing is not Christ-centric, it is eccentric, off-center and spiritually out of balance. Ministry can be an idol if it displaces our love and intimacy with the Lord as the main devotion of our life. What husband who passionately loves his wife would be pleased if his wife was so busy working for him that he never got to see her?

Many in ministry fall to worshipping the temple of the Lord more than the Lord of the temple. This is idolatry. Even the church, or "the great commission" can become idols if they displace Christ as the center of our devotion. We may say that our devotion to the things of God is a result of our love for God, but that is just an attempt to justify our deception. As the Lord warned the Ephesians church, if we lose our first love we are in jeopardy of losing everything.

Does this mean that we should just shut down all of our projects and programs to seek the Lord? For some, that is the only option if they ever hope to get back on the right track. However, that is not the solution for everyone. In ministry, once we take the wrong road it will never turn into the right road; the only way that we can get back on the right road is to go back to where we missed the turn.

If we missed the turn at the beginning of our ministry, that is where we must go back to. If we deviated somewhere along the way, that is where we need to return to get back on the right track. Many simply allowed the pressures of the ministry to push them off at some point, or succumbed to the "tyranny of the urgent." But if we have gotten off track we must turn around and go back to where we missed—this is called repentance.

Start at the Beginning

Paul explained to the Ephesians that there was only one foundation that could be laid. His discourse continues:

> **Now if any man builds upon the foundation with gold, silver, precious stones, wood, hay, straw,**
> **each man's work will become evident; for the day will show it, because it is to be revealed with fire; and the fire itself will test the quality of each man's work.**
> **If any man's work which he has built upon it remains, he shall receive a reward.**
> **If any man's work is burned up, he shall suffer loss; but he himself shall be saved, yet so as through fire (I Corinthians 3:12-15).**

Why should we go on building something if we know that it is going to be burned up? As Francis Frangipane once said, "The Lord inspects His house by walking through it and throwing matches!" I have heard many pastors describe their ministry as that of a fireman who just runs around putting out fires. Why not let them burn? A good many of them are being started by the Lord, and we are only hindering His work by putting them out. It is better that they burn now than after we have devoted a lifetime to the work—only to find that it did not pass the Lord's test.

This is not to imply that we should not address, or confront and try to solve problems in the church. However, we must use wisdom in this. Just as brush fires can help clean out the underbrush and debris in a forest and help prepare for new growth, some of the "fires" that sweep through our congregations really do help. They help by purging unnecessary entanglements and growth that will never bear fruit for the kingdom, but are in fact sapping the life out of our churches. We will only discern which fires are which if we have kept our focus on the ultimate purpose of God. Then we will quickly see those which will result in more Christlikeness.

In ministry we cannot be the Head of the church, and we cannot be the Holy Spirit to the church. We are co-laborers with Christ, but we are not here to do His work. He will build His church. We really can relax and enjoy it.

The foundation of any work is our relationship with Him. In construction, if the foundation is not level, the higher you build, the further off plumb the building will get. If you keep going higher there is a point at which it will collapse. If we have mislaid the foundation, we have no choice but to level the building and start over. If we laid a proper foundation, but improperly constructed one of the floors, we will have to rebuild that floor or everything that is built from that point up will be in jeopardy.

The wise master builder cannot tolerate inferior materials or procedures at any level. We must constantly examine everyone that we use and everything that is built for one quality—Christlikeness. As ministers of Christ we have a most holy commission that must not be compromised. **"If any man destroys the temple of God, God will destroy him, for the temple of God is holy, and that is what you are" (I Corinthians 3:17).**

As ministers of the gospel we are called as both ambassadors of the greatest kingdom, and master builders of the highest commission. Let us continually beseech the God of the resurrection, who Himself submitted unto death and was raised up by the glory of the Father, to give us the power of His resurrection life each day. This is not only so that we can preach the resurrection, but that our lives would be a demonstration of His resurrection life.

We must have living words that have sprung up from the Living Word Himself. The single most important action that any spiritual leader can take for his people is to get closer to the Lord Himself. If we are doing that, everything else will work out. If we are not doing that, everything else will continue to be burned up, regardless of how much we try to save it.

Jesus is the Crown of Glory. He is the Head of the church. All authority and power has been given to Him. We will only have true authority and power to the degree that we abide in Him. He is everything that the Father loves and esteems. All things were made through Him and for Him. In everything that was created the Father was looking for His Son's likeness. He is looking for His Son in us, and in all that we build in His name. Nothing else will last. He is our goal. Until we are like Him and do the works that He did, we are not finished. The Holy Spirit was given to us to lead us to Him. When we cease to pursue Him we have departed from the way, and the Source of our power.

CHAPTER THREE

The Seven Basic Truths

Therefore leaving the elementary teaching about the Christ, let us press on to maturity, not laying again a foundation of repentance from dead works and of faith toward God,

of instructions about washings, and laying on of hands, and the resurrection of the dead, and eternal judgment (Hebrews 6:1-2).

In this text we find listed the seven basic doctrines of Christianity. First is the "teaching about the Christ." Second is "repentance." Third is "faith toward God." Fourth is "instructions about washings." Fifth is "laying on of hands." Sixth is "the resurrection of the dead." The seventh is "eternal judgment." The strength with which these basic truths are established in the church will determine the basic strength of the church. However, it is hard to find a church that has more than just a cursory understanding of more than one or two of these basic truths.

This text begins with, **"Therefore leaving the elementary teaching about the Christ."** We must understand that this verse is not exhorting us to leave the teachings about Christ, but the *elementary* teachings about Him. We never outgrow the teachings about Christ. There is a saying that whenever you see a "therefore" in Scripture you should back up and see what it is *there for*. The verses preceding this "therefore" obviously relates to this text, as they read:

For though by this time you ought to be teachers, you have need again for someone to teach you the

elementary principles of the oracles of God, and you have come to need milk and not solid food.

For everyone who partakes only of milk is not accustomed to the word of righteousness, for he is a babe.

But solid food is for the mature, who because of practice have their senses trained to discern good and evil (Hebrews 5:12-14).

Here we are encouraged to "not lay again a foundation of repentance." However, it is understood that this exhortation is for those who have properly laid a foundation of repentance from dead works. It is the weakness of this part of the foundation of Christianity that is the likely source for the weakness of the modern church. The quality of our repentance is a factor that will determine the true quality and depth of our spiritual life. This is a foundation, and the strength of our foundation will determine the quality and strength of everything that is built upon it.

John the Baptist had to preach repentance before Jesus could be revealed. Without repentance the people never would have been able to recognize the Messiah, much less to receive Him. Repentance is a foundation of the true Christian life. Until the guilt of our sin becomes too unbearable and weighty for us to carry, we simply will not turn to the cross. Repentance is the confession of failure and the cry for help. Therefore repentance is the evidence of spiritual humility, and God only gives His grace to the humble (see James 4:6).

Human philosophies have offered many types of relief from guilt, and many of them will temporarily relieve the symptoms of our deadly spiritual disease, but the cross alone can cure us. When we try to relieve the symptoms of sin, such as guilt and depression, without confronting the cause of those symptoms, the deadly disease of sin, we only cover up the cancer so that it can grow unhindered. The cross uses the symptoms to lead us to the disease, and then it delivers us from the guilt and depression by killing the disease. Jesus did not just come to save us from death or hell; He came to save us from what is causing the death and hell.

Foundations Are Critical

There have been studies made that indicate a strong link between the nature of the birth and the course of the child's life. For example, when the philosophy of childbirth was promulgated that has been called, "drug them and tug them," which was to drug the mother and pull the baby out, the first generation born by the widespread use of this procedure became the first to widely use drugs. Such studies are general and obviously do not apply to every individual, but they do suggest overall trends.

This correlation is also found in relation to spiritual births. Those who are born into the kingdom through a radical conviction of sin, through great and difficult travail over their spiritual condition and the need for salvation, inevitably become the strongest, most radical, and most effective Christians. Likewise, those who are born again as the result of a weak gospel message tend to be weak and perpetually in need of ministry.

The Shackles of Sin

But how can we help the conditions under which we were born? It is true that we had nothing to do with the quality of the message preached that brought us into the kingdom. We had nothing to do with the state of the church, our mother. In a sense, she has been using spiritual "drugs" to make the birth process as painless as possible. These drugs are the doctrines of delusion that we are subject to when we are more concerned about feeling good than knowing the truth.

Perhaps it is not our fault that we were born into the church while she was in this state. So why are we being condemned for what we were not in control of? The apostle Paul succinctly answered this same question, **"Will the clay say to the potter, 'Why have you made me like this?'"** **(Romans 9:20).** This may be a valid question, maybe even an excuse, but to use it only strengthens the shackles of our sin, which perpetuates weakness and death in our lives.

The first result of the first sin was self-centeredness. Adam and Eve looked at themselves and saw that they were naked. The next result was blame-shifting. Adam blamed the woman, which God had given to Him, effectively putting the blame back on God for his sin. The woman blamed the serpent for her sin, and since God was the one who allowed it in the Garden, it must all be His fault, thus relieving her of any responsibility. Such excuses may make us feel better about ourselves for a time, but they make our deliverance from the problem impossible.

The recovery of personal responsibility is the first step that must be taken for salvation to come. God does not forgive excuses; He forgives sin. The first evidence that true salvation is working in us is that we stop looking at ourselves and start looking to God. The second evidence is that we stop blaming everyone else for our problems and start confessing them as sins.

It is true that we may have had nothing to do with the condition of our birth. We did not choose to be born into this world in such a fallen condition. We can stand on this fact to our eternal dismay, or we can seize the salvation that has so graciously been provided for us. We may want to blame our potty training for all of our problems; we can blame parents, teachers, brothers, sisters, or other Christians for our problems—we have probably suffered injustices from all of them.

There may be genuine reasons for us to be the way we are. We can hang onto our excuses, and our sin, or we can be freed, and be made into new creatures who bear the glorious image of Christ. We will never be freed until we take our eyes off of ourselves and look to Him, until we stop blame-shifting and confess our own sins.

A great grace is coming that is going to allow many who have been both improperly born and raised spiritually to rebuild their foundations. This does not mean that everything in their spiritual experience is useless and must be discarded, but a great renewal is coming to strengthen the whole body of Christ by replacing delusions with the power of the cross. This can only be done on the true foundation of repentance.

Once a foundation is laid, it is not that we do not use it again, but rather the whole building can only stand as long as it remains strong. We do not lay the foundation again in the sense that we do not put a foundation on top of the second or third stories, but the foundation is used every day that the building is used. We never stop repenting when we need to, but once a strong and clear understanding of it becomes a part of our life, we do not need to keep teaching it, or laying again that foundation.

Pain Is a Friend

A good conscience that pangs us with guilt is one of the most needed ingredients for a healthy spiritual life. Such a conscience is really a sensitivity to the Holy Spirit. One of His primary duties is to convict the world of sin. Those who are no longer convicted by their sin are in the most dangerous condition of having a seared conscience that no longer responds to the Holy Spirit.

It is easy to understand how modern medicine would want to relieve pain that they deem unnecessary. Even human compassion is moved to do all that can be done to remove pain from the world. However, pain has a most important place in the present state of the world, and to alleviate it can sometimes be very dangerous. As the proverb states, **"Faithful are the wounds of a friend, but deceitful are the kisses of an enemy" (Proverbs 27:6).** Pain is an alarm that something is wrong and needs correction. It is the shallowness of our present state that has made pain the enemy. Pain is a friend that is trying to warn us about the real problem.

Spiritual pain is caused by the conviction of sin. Freud was right when he discerned that guilt was the cause of most of the depression and neurosis afflicting the world. However, he released more depression and a deeper neurosis upon the world when he began attacking the guilt instead of the cause of the guilt—sin! If we remove the guilt before the sin is removed, it is like relieving a headache that is caused by brain cancer so that the tumor can grow undetected.

We are guilty, and it is right that we feel guilt until we have been to the cross to have it relieved. I am not okay and you are not okay. We are in desperate need of help, and the cross is the only place that we can find it. The cross is the power of God, it is the only provision for salvation, deliverance or healing. If we are to know the power of God in our daily lives we must take up our crosses daily.

Going to the cross is painful, but it is the only place where the pain can truly be relieved. Once we have been crucified with Christ there is no greater freedom from pain that we can know. It must be our goal as Christians to relieve the guilt and pain, but not by removing the symptoms, but by removing that which is causing them—sin.

The reality with which we face our sin in the beginning of our Christian life will almost certainly dictate the reality with which we will face our entire lives. That reality will have much to do with the degree of truth that we walk in. I did not say the degree of truth that we *know*, but the degree of truth that we *walk in*. The basic definition of a hypocrite is one who knows the truth but does not live it. The Lord reserved His most scathing condemnation for the hypocrites because that is the most dangerous state that we can find ourselves in.

A Barometer of Our Condition

There is reason to both rejoice and be sobered by the testimonies of healings and deliverance of those who have been touched by the present move of the Spirit popularly known as "the Toronto blessing." We should be sobered by the fact that so many Christians, many of whom have been in the faith for many years, still needed such deliverance.

Many of the testimonies of deliverance from depression, bitterness, hatreds, etc., were from men and women who have been Christians for twenty or thirty years! Why is it taking so many so long to receive deliverance from those things that we should have been freed of when we were born again? When we are born again **"all things are become new" (II Corinthians 5:17 KJV).** If all things have become new, there is no longer a reason to feel rejected or resentful about our past.

How can we who have been given such a glorious future in Christ, eternal life in the splendors of heaven, who have been given angels as ministers, be so concerned about such pettiness in this temporary realm? It can only be because we are still earthly minded, which the apostle explained would only result in death (see Romans 8:6). Why do we still choose death over life? Why do we go on eating from the Tree of the Knowledge of Good and Evil when the Tree of Life is available to us?

It is right to rejoice when anyone is delivered from the shackles of sin such as bitterness or depression, but we must also be sobered by the fact that we need so much of it. The church is, generally, in a very low state. The ultimate vision of many is to just get to the place that a new Christian should be walking in from the time he was born again. *We are called to be a "new creation" that greatly exceeds the original creation before the fall.*

We have been given something much greater than just walking with God in the Garden, or even walking with Jesus when He walked upon the earth—we have Him living inside of us! The same power that created the universe is in even the youngest Christian. If just one Christian starts to walk in the reality of what we have been given, the whole world will be shocked into soberness, quickly. The apostle Paul stated it this way:

But if the ministry of death, in letters engraved on stones, came with glory, so that the sons of Israel

**could not look intently at the face of Moses because
of the glory of his face, fading as it was,**
   **how shall the ministry of the Spirit fail to be even
more with glory? (II Corinthians 3:7-8).**

Paul is clearly saying that normal, New Covenant ministry
should come with even more glory than that which Moses
experienced, and he had to put a veil over his face because it
was so great. Where is the glory in the church? Who could claim
to have experienced even the glory that Moses did? This clearly
indicates that there is much more available than we are presently walking in.

Our goal should be much more than just having healthy,
happy lives. We are called to be bearers of the glory of God. We
are called to challenge even the greatest darkness of our times,
and to push it back. We are here to tear down the enemy's
strongholds, and to set the captives free. All that is now happening is wonderful, but we must never lose the vision for
something that is much greater than anything that we are yet
seeing. We must not camp here, but we must keep going higher.
Let us never stop praying what has become one of the great
prophetic prayers of our times—MORE LORD!

The present renewal movement is not taking the church to
new ground, but it is helping multitudes of believers take back
ground that has been lost. It is already a movement of historic
significance, but it is already beginning to peak and subside.
This is not a defeat, but a sign that the job has been done. It is
now time to go forward. Once the army is healed it is time to
march. If we do not go on to higher ground, we will sink back
to an even lower state. But that will only happen if we refuse
to hear the clear trumpet call that is already being sounded.

The bride of the Lamb is more awesome than an army with
banners (see Song of Solomon 6:4, 10). The banners of her
great companies are now being unfurled all over the earth.
When she begins to march again the earth will tremble at the
sound of it. Let us not be left behind. Regardless of how you

may have been hurt by church relationships in the past, get healed and get back in the ranks. The awesome day of the Lord is certainly very near.

Building on the Foundation

Once we have laid a strong foundation of repentance in our life, and have a solid understanding of the other basic truths of the faith that are listed in Hebrews 6:1-2, we must go on to more solid spiritual food. It is a wonderful thing to be born again, but being born is just the beginning of life. We must go on to maturity. We must set our vision on the purpose for which we have been made a new creation.

Abraham rejoiced when Isaac was born, but he threw a great feast when he was weaned. Heaven rejoices at every new birth, but it also rejoices when we grow up. Again, until we are like Jesus, and do the works that He did, we are not there yet.

CHAPTER FOUR

Resurrection Life

Charles Spurgeon once made this remarkable statement; "There are very few Christians who believe in the resurrection." How could someone be a Christian and not believe in the resurrection? As I pondered this I began to understand that this is probably true. There is a difference between giving intellectual, or doctrinal assent to the fact of the resurrection and having faith in it. There is a difference between believing in our minds and believing in our hearts. *If we really believed in our hearts the truth of the resurrection our lives would be radically different.*

The delusion that mere intellectual agreement with certain biblical and historical facts is true faith has caused many to feel safe in a spiritual condition in which their eternal lives may still be in jeopardy. The apostle Paul made this clear:

> **If you confess with your mouth Jesus as Lord, *and believe in your heart* that God raised Him from the dead, you shall be saved;**
> **for with *the heart* man believes, resulting in right-eousness (Romans 10:9-10).**

Funk & Wagnals Standard Handbook of Synonyms, Antonyms & Prepositions defines *faith* as "a union of belief and trust; *it is a belief so strong that it becomes a part of one's own nature."* This is not to imply that Funk & Wagnals has the authority to establish doctrine, but knowing the definition of our words is important, and this definition of faith certainly applies.

Faith is stronger than belief. To believe is to give intellectual assent; to have faith is to be inseparable from the object of your devotion. Belief can be changed or lost by a more persuasive argument. True faith is so much a part of the person it can only be taken by death. Faith is the substance of our very existence and identity; our faith is who we are. The stronger our faith, the more impact we will have in this world. The more positive the faith, the more edifying this impact will be.

This difference between "belief" and "faith" is the difference between being true and a mere pretender who has deluded himself in order to appease his conscience. The popular and pervasive "believing in God," that is just believing that He exists, accomplishes little and is not the true Christian "faith." The concept that we just need to believe that He exists is a delusion that keeps us from the true religion of faith *in* God.

A person without true faith is like a car without an engine. It may have a beautiful appearance but it will not get you any-where. The stronger the faith the further and the faster we will go. Belief alone is superficial and accomplishes little more than appeasing the emotions. Faith is a living power that can move the mountains that stand in the way of its goal.

The Forge of Faith

Moses led the Israelites into the wilderness in order to convert their superstitions and shallow beliefs into a rock solid faith. Your wilderness, or the trials that you are enduring to test your faith, is meant to accomplish the same for you. If you respond properly to your wilderness it will turn mere emo-tional frivolity into a force! Embrace your difficulties as oppor-tunities and you *will* get to your promised land. Let the difficulties discourage you and you will not realize your goal and purpose in the Lord.

Moses could lead Israel out of Egypt but he could not take Egypt out of the Israelites; the difficulties of the wilderness were meant to do that. The Israelites had been slaves in Egypt, which is the most base human condition. As difficult as it may be to understand, there is a security in slavery which is hard to get free of. Even though the Israelites were freed and moving toward their destiny and fulfillment, when they encountered difficulties most of them began looking back on the terrible oppression of slavery and wanted to return to it.

Herein lies the dividing line that separates those who go on to victory from those who go back to their doom. No one will attain his goal or destiny until he becomes *free*. The free man would rather perish in the wilderness trying to fulfill his destiny than go back to slavery. Until we make the decision that we will not go back, we will not go forward. Jesus once declared, **"No one, who puts his hand to the plow and looks back is fit for service in the kingdom of God" (Luke 9:62 NIV).**

The most telltale symptom of surrender to slavery is *grumbling* and *complaining*. The one who complains has lost the faith; he has already given up in his heart. The one with true faith meets obstacles as opportunities to win a greater victory and make a greater advance toward his goal. This cannot be blind optimism which is just another form of mere intellectual assessment masquerading as true faith. Optimism will wither in the heat of the desert wilderness, but true faith becomes stronger and more determined as the heat is increased.

Faith Makes the Way

Faith is able to move mountains, and it will move every one that stands in its way. True faith makes the road; it does not follow one. That is why true faith is true freedom; *no* shackle can be put on it. True faith is the ability to seize the vision of one's destiny with such a grip that it cannot be taken away until it is fulfilled. Such faith moves every obstacle, but is moved by no obstacle. True faith *will* get to the promised land.

The Israelites began to complain when they finally came to a well and found the waters to be bitter. They did not understand that God intended to turn the bitter waters into sweet as an object lesson. Their first response to the disappointment was doubt and complaining. Because of this the destroyer was released among them.

Everyone who has been truly thirsty can identify with the Israelites. Real thirst arouses our basic instincts of survival. They may have had a real good excuse for complaining, but this difficult test was also their greatest opportunity. It is the real test that brings out real faith.

True faith is internal, not external and it is not dependent on external circumstances. True faith is not altered by disappointment; it is strengthened. It will always turn the bitter waters of disappointment into the sweet waters of opportunity. When disappointment results in complaining the destroyer of our faith has been released and our vision will become clouded.

It is important to understand that true faith *is not* a faith in one's faith! True faith has an Object and a Source of its power which is greater than one's self. *True faith is not in the quality of our faith; true faith is in God!* Anything less is worse than a pretension; it is deception. Inevitably, those whose faith is in themselves only accomplish that which is selfish. Self-centeredness opened the first door to deception, and will always lead to it.

The Bible settles this issue at the beginning. After Adam and Eve listened to Satan's advice and ate of the forbidden fruit, the first fruit of their sin was that they immediately began to focus upon themselves and noticed their own nakedness. The self-centered are the most emotionally crippled, not to mention boring, mere shells of what the human being is meant to be. When we start looking to ourselves we will fall from the grace and power of true faith.

Stephen Hawking is reputedly one of the greatest thinkers of our time. He is considered by some to be an even greater theorist than Einstein. He is said to have the potential to grasp answers to questions which other great scientists have not yet even been able to ask. He said that his quest for knowledge is simply "trying to understand the mind of God."

Finding that *Reason* for our lives, which is to find the mind of God, is the Object and Source of all true faith. Anything less than seeking the Purpose that is *ordained* is sub-human and not worthy of intelligent expenditure of energy or time. Only when we find *God's* plan and possess it with the true faith will we be fulfilled.

This is the brilliance of the apostle who exhorted us to **"study to show yourselves approved unto God,"** *not men* **(II Timothy 2:15** KJV**).** When we have direction which we know is from the Source, a power is released called *faith* that nothing in the rest of creation can hinder. There is no greater motivation than knowing our destiny, and there is no greater power available than that which is found in the resolve of those who are seizing theirs.

False Faith

Sadly, one of the greatest obstacles to understanding and believing the Christian faith has been the church. This is because much of the visible church has become an example of how shallow belief continually attempts to usurp the position of true faith. The faith of the apostles was devoted to building a temple for God that could not be made with human hands, which could only be contained in human hearts. The church they preached was made of people who had true faith. The church they preached about was not an organization but a living organism; it was not an institution but a constitution.

The apostolic vision was God living in people—not bricks. Just as shallow men used the profound discoveries of Einstein to build the most terrible vehicles of destruction (bombs), shallow religious men have reduced the true faith to empty rituals and form that destroys men's souls. When one grasps the true faith he does not go to church; *he becomes the church.* The true church is a source of power and life that no building or institution can contain—only the human heart is great enough when it has been purified by faith.

Reality is not found in ritual. True faith is a river of life too powerful to be contained in the weak structures men have tried to construct. Certainly gatherings of those who share a real faith and the power of that faith, and some of these gatherings *are* found in institutional churches.

If you ever possess real faith you will be drawn to the most real people who live on this earth. There is a strengthening we all receive when we are joined to others with true faith. But true faith does not worship the temple of God; it worships the God of the temple. When those with the true faith are asked about their faith they do not point to a building or organization, to doctrines or even concepts about truth—they point to the True God.

The apostle Paul explained that, **"The kingdom of God does not consist in words, but in power" (I Corinthians 4:20).** The apostles and prophets foresaw a house of true faith, not being built *by* people but being built *out of people.* If you become one of those spiritual stones assembled to contain this power, you will easily recognize others who are also a part of the same.

We cannot recognize such just by creeds or alliances, but by the power and the character of the One who has imparted the true faith to them. Church is not something we go to; it is something we become. We must not continue to settle for anything less than that which is ultimately true. Good is often the worst enemy of best.

Faith Is Power

It was reported that when Napoleon read the Gospel of John he declared that either Jesus was the Son of God or the one who wrote this gospel was! Napoleon recognized that the genius of true Christianity was far beyond the creative powers of any mere human intellect. He then looked at the institution of Christianity and saw no relationship to the Jesus in that gospel.

There often is no relationship between the substance of truth and what men try to do with it. Just as it was the most religious and upstanding citizens who crucified Jesus, it is the most religious and upstanding institutions that often destroy true faith in Him.

But true faith will not die in an institution. It is an indestructible power that was able to transform even a few fishermen and humble folk into the greatest force in history. It challenged and defeated the greatest empire in history and unraveled it, with but a few epistles written from prison. It was the power of true faith that took those same letters written by these simple people, and impacted history more than all other books combined have been able to do. Just a small portion of this true faith in our life will so radically transform us that any one person who has it can do the same.

Martin Luther was just a monk, living in an obscure little town in an obscure province. His church was hardly as big as the typical American garage. Yet this humble man who discovered the Source, faith, challenged the greatest darkness of his time and pushed it back. No conqueror in all of history impacted the course of the world to the degree that this monk did. He is one of the greatest testimonies of the power of even the most humble man, who will take his stand on the truth and refuse to compromise, to redirect the entire course of history.

The truth that we have been entrusted with is more powerful than any lie. It is greater than any other power found on the earth. From the most noble and far reaching human ideals to the biggest nuclear device, nothing in all of history has demonstrated the power to change history like truth united with faith.

But we must beware! Only the most courageous have pressed beyond the muddied waters of pretend faith to taste the pure waters of the true. It was meant to be that way. The power of the true faith is too great to entrust to anyone who will not esteem it as his most precious possession and pay the price to get it. Such is the constitution of all who would rise above mediocrity to the highest place. The wilderness is meant to bring out the best, or the worst, in us. We decide which it will be.

The Test of Faith

Paul implored the Corinthians to **"Test yourselves to see if you are in the faith; examine yourselves!" (II Corinthians 13:5).** The overemphasis upon *what* we believe instead of *how* we believe has resulted in many becoming more like parrots than like Christ. We can say the right things, and even do the right things, but if our hearts are not changed, we are living in a delusion. Faith changes the heart.

In Acts 1:22 we see that the apostolic office was for the purpose of being *"a witness of His resurrection."* The faith and power of the biblical church was the result of their faith in the resurrection, *but so was the persecution they experienced.* When Peter and John were dragged before the Sanhedrin it was because the rulers were **"being greatly disturbed because they [Peter and John] were teaching the people and proclaiming in Jesus** *the resurrection from the dead"* (Acts 4:2). When Paul was later arrested and brought before this same council, he declared, **"I am on trial for the hope and resurrection of the dead!"** (Acts 23:6).

There may be little we can do that will bring persecution upon us faster than preaching the message of the resurrection. This is because when we begin to preach this message we are attacking Satan's most powerful stronghold in the human heart—*the fear of death.* There is no truth that will set us more free than the truth of the resurrection. When we are released from this fear, we will be free indeed. This freedom is a prerequisite to complete freedom in any other area of our lives. The witness of the resurrection had to be the basic message of the apostolic gospel.

The Father of Faith

Have you ever wondered why more of the Bible is devoted to Abraham finding a burial place than to such important subjects as being born again? Why did Isaac and Jacob insist on being buried in the same place? Why would Joseph make Israel swear to carry up his bones to bury him in the same place? And why was that listed in Hebrews chapter eleven as one of the great acts of faith? What difference did it make where they were buried? We see the answer when we read the account of the crucifixion of Jesus in Matthew:

And Jesus cried out again with a loud voice, and yielded up His spirit.

And behold, the veil of the temple was torn in two from top to bottom, and the earth shook; and the rocks were split,

and the tombs were opened; *and many bodies of the saints who had fallen asleep were raised* **(Matthew 27:50-52).**

These men had prophetically foreseen the crucifixion and resurrection of Jesus and had positioned themselves to be a part of it. The Lord Himself confirmed this when He said, **"Your father Abraham rejoiced to see My day, and he** *saw* **it and was glad" (John 8:56).**

When the "eyes of our hearts" are opened we begin to see the things that are eternal and we are no longer bound by time and by the things which are temporal. Abraham saw with the eyes of His heart. Therefore, he could look ahead to see the crucifixion and resurrection of Jesus and believe in Him just like we do looking back in history.

When we begin to see with the eyes of our hearts instead of just our natural eyes, we begin to see the things that are eternal, and they become *more real* to us than the things which are temporary. Then, like Abraham, we do not become overly possessive of anything in the temporary realm. Even the chosen purpose of God in our life, our "Isaacs," we will freely give back to God because we know that the resurrection will give them back to us for eternity.

Because Abraham had seen the day of the Lord he understood that Isaac was a "type" (see Hebrews 11:19) or prophetic model of the coming Messiah. That is why he made Isaac carry the wood for his own sacrifice just as Jesus was to bear His own cross. That is why he could so confidently say, **"God will provide for Himself the lamb" (Genesis 22:8).** When we have the eyes of our hearts opened to see the purpose and plan of God, a faith is imparted to live radically different and free from the bonds of temporal concerns.

But how do we get this faith so that the eyes of our hearts are opened? How do we get our intellectual understanding of biblical truths transferred from our minds to our hearts? The answer to this question is utterly practical: begin to develop a *secret* relationship with God. Jesus asked His followers, **"How can you believe, when you receive glory from one another, and you do not seek the glory that is from the one and only God?" (John 5:44).** This statement highlighted the fact that one of the most destructive factors undermining true faith is our desire for human recognition. The Lord also warned:

> **Beware of practicing your righteousness before men to be noticed by them;** *otherwise you have no reward with your Father who is in heaven.*
>
> **When therefore you give alms, do not sound a trumpet before you, as the hypocrites do in the synagogues and the streets, that they may be honored by men. Truly I say to you, they have their reward in full.**
>
> **But when you give alms, do not let your left hand know what your right hand is doing**
>
> **that your alms may be in secret; and your Father** *who sees in secret* **will repay you.**
>
> **And when you pray, you are not to be as the hypocrites; for they love to stand and pray in the synagogues and on the street corners, in order to be seen by men. Truly I say to you, they have their reward in full.**
>
> **But you, when you pray, go into your inner room, and when you have shut your door,** *pray to your Father*

who is in secret, and your Father who sees in secret will repay you **(Matthew 6:1-6).**

Some of the most devoted servants, the most faithful intercessors and the most generous contributors to the Lord's purposes have, for their actions, little or no heavenly reward, because they have sought mere human recognition for them on earth. When we do this we receive our reward "in full." If we really believed in the resurrection and understood that we are laying up fruit for eternal life, we would not be wasting an eternal inheritance on such trivial and fleeting human recognition and honor.

On the other hand, when we begin to believe the resurrection in our hearts, we become increasingly focused on laying up fruit for eternal life. We will begin to build that secret relationship with the Father, not wanting anyone but our Father to know about our alms or prayers. When we do this, and our treasure really is being deposited in our "heavenly bank account": where our treasure, is there will our heart be also. *When our hearts are with the Father in heaven, the eyes of our hearts start to open and those things which are eternal become more real to us than the things which are passing away.* That is precisely the nature of true faith.

There is some truth to the seed faith teachings, but when we begin to set our eyes on things above instead of things on earth, we do not give in order to get a bigger house or better car; we give in order to get more to give for the sake of this glorious gospel. Those who have set their affections on things above do not want to cash the checks from their spiritual bank account on that which is temporal; they would rather give it to the work of bringing more souls into the kingdom of God.

Laying aside the hope of *our* reward, once we have fully comprehended what Jesus did for us, we will want to do it all for Him. Our passion will be to see Him receive the reward of His sacrifice. When we see what He has done for us, how can we be selfishly ambitious with even our heavenly treasures?

Even so, by the Lord's grace, He has purchased us and made us slaves (as we are to no longer live for ourselves, but for Him—see II Corinthians 5:15), and yet He pays us better than any human agency ever could. And when we give ourselves to the support of others, we partake of their fruit *forever*!

When we really begin to believe in the resurrection and the eternal inheritance we have in Christ, there is no place for jealousy or territorial preservation. If someone comes to your town with a greater anointing, pray for him. Find out how you can support him, because then you can partake of the fruit of his ministry for eternity. You will then hope that he will be more "successful," because you too will be partaking of the reward of his ministry. When we see this we will begin to watch over and protect one another's ministries instead of trying to undermine them or to tear them down.

It is not wrong to obey for the reward; even Jesus endured the cross **"for the joy set before Him" (Hebrews 12:2).** Obeying for the sake of the reward is not a wrong or evil motive, but there are more noble motives that we will have as our love for the Lord grows. The Lord's joy for which He endured the cross was basically His desire to obey and please the Father. This was also the joy that He knew that we would enjoy with Him.

One of the chief joys we will ever receive will be to hear the Lord say to us on that day: "Well done good and faithful servant," and to see the joy He receives from the redemption of those for whom we labored. It is the joy of the Lord, not just our joy, that is the ultimate source of our strength and purpose. We can bring Him joy today by believing in Him, in His resurrection, and by devoting ourselves to that secret relationship He wants to have with each one of us.

CHAPTER FIVE

God's Ultimate Plan

Repent therefore and return, that your sins may be wiped away, in order that times of refreshing may come from the presence of the Lord;

and that He may send Jesus, the Christ appointed for you,

whom heaven must receive *until the period of restoration of all things* about which God spoke by the mouth of His holy prophets from ancient time (Acts 3:19-21).

The first two chapters in the Bible combined with the last two make a complete story. Everything between those four chapters deals with essentially one subject—restoring man and the creation to the place from which they have fallen. The process by which the Lord accomplishes this restoration is called redemption. Understanding redemption is fundamental to understanding all that God has done, is doing, or will do on the earth, from the Fall until the earth is fully restored.

The New Creation

In the midst of God's great and epic plan to redeem His fallen creation, He determined to take what the enemy intended for evil and turn it into an even greater good. Those who participate with Him in His plan of redemption are enabled to become a "new creation," which greatly transcends the original creation.

We may think that there would be nothing more wonderful than to have the kind of relationship with God that Adam had before the Fall. However, the Lord told His disciples that it was actually better for them if He departed this life so that the Holy Spirit could come to live in them. By this He was saying that the gift of the indwelling Holy Spirit was to be esteemed above walking in the flesh with Jesus, the man.

Through the new creation the gap between the spiritual and natural realms has been bridged. Men who are flesh can actually become partakers of the divine nature through Christ. Though we walk on the earth, we can be seated with Him in the heavenly places. In the original, uncorrupted creation, God walked with man and had fellowship with him. In the new creation God has come to live *in* man, calling us to be His eternal dwelling place. This is a much higher calling.

Every Christian has the One who knows all things and controls all things living within him. This must be one of the greatest marvels to all creation, from the angels in heaven to the demons in hell. Why would God esteem men so as to choose us to be His temple? This may be even more difficult for us, who are a part of the fallen race, to understand, knowing our own corruption and tendency toward evil. Even so, once we, who deserve it so little, come to this understanding, we appreciate it even more. Those who are forgiven much will love much.

However, we cannot behold or become a part of this new creation without understanding, partaking of, and being a part of the implementation of the basic plan of redemption. The high calling of God to be a part of His new creation is a call to service. Servanthood is a prerequisite for this calling. The higher the calling the more we are called to serve. Reconciling the world back to God is our basic ministry. Man turned from God but God never turned from man. He even gave His own life for man, and all who are called to be His ambassadors must do the same.

How many of us, if we knew that all of our best friends, those for whom we had poured out our life for over three years, were going to desert us and even deny that they knew us, would still earnestly desire to have a last meal with them? After all that the Lord put into preparing the twelve, only one of them would be found at the base of the cross, standing with Him in His time of greatest need. Yet, the Lord never gave up on the others, and He never condemned them for failing Him so.

The Bible is not a story about men who sought God, but about the way that God has sought men. Through all of the rebellion and rebuffs that men have given to Him, He has never given up on us. That is His nature, and it must also be ours if we are to be in unity with Him.

If we are going to be in unity with the Lord in His plan of redemption, we must learn to look past the failures of one another. Since the first century, the history of great men of God has far too often been that of great exploits only to be followed by a great fall at the end.

The leaders of almost every great move of God have ended up persecuting the movements that followed them. There has hardly been an exception to this. The great men of Scripture often endured many failures, but ended in triumph. Since then, leaders have had many great successes, only to end too often in tragic defeat and delusion. We are reaping tragedy for the way we have abused our fallen brethren. Rather than extending grace and mercy, the way that the Lord did, we often condemn them to a spiritual graveyard and have nothing else to do with them. Is this the example that the Lord left for us?

Why He's Coming Back

When the Lord returns to "restore all things," He will come with a rod of iron to swiftly punish those who do not obey. However, that time has not yet come. Sin is not swiftly punished, but rather rewarded by the present ruler of this evil age.

Satan still offers to the Lord's people what he offered to Jesus two thousand years ago. Satan does reward those who bow down to him, who will live according to his ways. It is in the midst of this evil environment that the Lord is choosing those who will be a part of His "new creation," who will be members of His own household and will reign with Him. This is the highest calling in the creation and their worship and obedience must be proven. Adam lived in a perfect world but still chose to disobey. Those of the new creation will have lived in a dark and evil world that rewards sin, but will have chosen to obey God against all of the pressures and influences of this evil age.

Jesus was **"the last Adam" (I Corinthians 15:45 KJV).** As Adam began the first race of men, Jesus also began a new race, a spiritual one. This new race transforms men from the first creation into a new race that is far greater than the first. However, the purpose of the new creation is the redemption of the first creation.

We must never forget that the Lord fully intends to "restore all things." This is the reason for His return. If He did not intend to restore the earth He would have just snatched us away to heaven and then destroyed the earth. He is coming back, and bringing us with Him, to rule over it until the restoration is complete.

When Jesus saw what was wrong with the world, He did not condemn it. It was already condemned, and He laid down His life for it. It is likewise the nature of those who are united to Him to lay down their lives to help restore those who are the slaves of this evil age. He knows that we will not be fully successful until He returns. One reason that He did not just snatch us away to heaven as soon as we committed our lives to follow Him was for our sakes—to learn, and to prove our devotion to Him and His purposes.

The Nature of Leaders

Right after the Lord said to Peter, **"Blessed are you, Simon Barjona, because flesh and blood did not reveal this to you, but My Father who is in heaven" (Matthew 16:17),** the Lord gave him the keys of the kingdom of heaven. His very next words to Peter were, **"Get behind Me, Satan!" (verse 23).** Right after Peter received a word straight from the Father he received one straight from the enemy. But even though Peter would fall hard at times, he would get up and keep going.

Therefore, even after his mistakes, the Lord did not take the keys to the kingdom away from him. In spite of his flaws, Peter, who would get out of the boat to walk on water, was the disciple most likely to use the keys to open the doors.

God does not tempt us, but He does test us. His tests are given for the purpose of qualifying us for promotions to the next grade, to give us more spiritual authority. Restoring our fallen brethren is a test that many of us will have to pass before we can go on. It is His intention to use some of the church's biggest embarrassments as testimonies of His power of redemption. We were all hurt by some of these public falls, which forces us to decide—do we really believe in forgiveness, and will we practice it, or will we just continue to preach it?

The Lord often tests us through His true vessels, separating those who really love the truth from those who judge by appearances. Jonah was also such a vessel, as were many of the other prophets in Scripture. We now esteem Isaiah, but how many of us would have identified ourselves with a prophet who went around naked for three and a half years? How many of us would have asked John the Baptist over for Sunday dinner? Would you have wanted to live next door to Hosea and his harlot wife? How many of us, had we been those with great religious influence, would really have been open to listen to a carpenter from Nazareth? In fact, almost all of God's vessels will bring major testing to the flesh, and those who trust in the arm of the flesh will not pass this testing.

God's Primary Business

Greater anointing and spiritual authority brings greater potential for deception and failure when a servant is given over to sin. The greater the anointing, the greater the blind spots that one is also likely to have. Even the greatest man of God is fallible, and if we ever think that we cannot fall we have probably already begun to. We must examine how and why our brothers and sisters have fallen, or we ourselves will be in danger of falling into the same traps. The only way that we can fully understand what happened to them will be through the process of restoration.

After King David fell into sin with Bathsheba, all of Israel went astray and followed after Absalom. It was probably very hard for the people of Israel to believe that someone who had fallen into such debauchery could still be anointed. However, the Lord was not surprised by what David did. He knew what was in David's heart when He called him. He knew that it was going to happen when He made him the King.

The Lord used David before the fall, and after it. We must understand that the primary business of our God at this time is redemption. Yet we who have been the recipients of His great grace often have the most difficulty in extending it to others. We must get this right if we are going to properly represent Him on this earth.

The Highest Calling

When all of Israel went astray and followed after Absalom, Zadok, the High Priest, picked up the Ark and followed David. He followed him at the risk of not only his ministry, but his life. Even if they were to survive, it appeared very unlikely that David would be restored to the throne. At best, those who followed him would probably spend the rest of their lives living in caves and holes in the ground as they had when being pursued by King Saul. Even so, Zadok was more faithful to the anointing than he was to political expediency, or to even his own welfare. He knew that, regardless of David's great sin, the anointing was still on him. Zadok simply followed God regardless of the cost.

God rewarded Zadok's courage and faithfulness with one of the greatest blessings recorded in the Scriptures. He was promised that his sons would minister to the Lord personally (see Ezekiel 40:46 & 44:15-16), essentially saying that they would be the closest to the Lord. When the Jews declared to Jesus that they were the sons of Abraham, He replied that if they were the sons of Abraham they would do the deeds of Abraham.

Likewise, those who are the true sons of Zadok are those who do the deeds of Zadok.

The true sons of Zadok are those who will follow the anointing regardless of the risk. They will follow the anointing, and the anointed, even when everyone else turns away. These are the spiritual sons of Zadok who will be the closest to the Lord and serve Him personally.

We will all have to choose between the anointing and respectability. Rising above spiritual politics to be faithful to what is right is one of the most important tests that anyone called to walk in spiritual authority must pass.

Will we, like King Saul, make our decisions based on the pressures of the people or the political consequences? Or will we, like King David, rise above the pressures of the people, or the circumstances of this world, to always seek the Lord's will first? A great demarcation always comes to the leadership of the church based on this one issue. Ultimately, every individual, church, movement, and many cities, will have to pass this test before they will be endorsed with the anointing that will be required by those who will be a part of the last day ministry of the church.

Restoration Is Not Optional

Galatians 6:1 states, **"If a man is caught in *ANY TRES-PASS,* you who are spiritual, *restore* such a one in a spirit of gentleness; each one looking to yourself, lest you too be tempted."** Regardless of how distasteful someone's sin may be to us personally, we are not given the choice as to whether or not we will restore him; if we do not, we ourselves come into jeopardy of falling to the same temptations. There is not a single one of us who stands to any degree except for the grace of God. If we cannot restore our fallen brothers and sisters, how can we preach redemption, reconciliation, and forgiveness to the world?

After his fall, King David rose to much greater heights of spiritual authority and prophetic revelation. So can all who have been tripped up by the enemy, or have been carried away with their own lusts. The Lord loves everyone of them. If we are in unity with Him should we not be desiring and seeking this for our fallen brothers? Those who are forgiven much, love much. God loves all men and sincerely desires for all to be saved. All that the enemy meant for evil the Lord intends to use as testimonies of His power of redemption.

Strangely, Christians often have more trouble forgiving each other than the heathen do. Understandably, we expect Christian leaders to have much higher standards of integrity and are therefore more shocked by their failures. Even so, we are all born into the failure of sin, and it is not easy for any of us to walk in continual freedom from its seductive clutches. Even so, we must believe in the Lord's forgiveness and power of redemption, before the world is going to believe us. Those who have fallen to various traps of the enemy, even "any trespass," must be restored or we will continue to be subject to the same temptations.

Restoring is more than just forgiving. We can apologize to these fallen brothers or sisters to appease our consciences, but that is not enough to pass the test. *They must be restored.* This does not imply in any way that the biblical standards of integrity should be compromised, or that restoration does not involve a process implemented over time. Even so, we must do whatever it takes for the fallen to be fully restored.

Our Father does not want any of His children left in the ditch by their brothers and sisters, but that is not the only reason why we are required to restore those who have fallen. It is only through the process of restoration that we will learn where the gates of hell are, and how to shut them. The gates of hell are the places that the enemy is using to gain access into the world, the church, and our own lives.

The Reward

It is true that we seldom pass God's tests with a perfect score. God's purpose is not bound up in our reputation, and we should all be thankful that He is not trying to be just or fair, but merciful. To be truly prophetic requires that, if we know that we are known by God and sent by Him, it really must not matter what anyone else thinks of us.

If we are going to be a prophetic people, and help restore a prophetic church, we must have the constitution of Elijah, who could even stand before the king and say, **"As the LORD, the God of Israel lives,** *before whom I stand . . ."* **(I Kings 17:1).** By this Elijah was saying, "I am not standing in front of you, Ahab. You're just a man. I stand before the living God. I live my life before God, not men." Until we have this attitude we will not be free to either love men properly, or to speak the truth to them without compromise, both of which are required of a true ministry.

It always takes humility for us to forgive, and to be able to restore and receive those who may have embarrassed us. Even so, there was only One in all of Scripture who did not embarrass the Lord. We have all fallen short, and we all need grace. Because we are promised that we will reap what we sow, the more grace we can sow toward others, the more we will receive ourselves. In fact, the Lord made it very clear that we will not be forgiven ourselves if we do not forgive.

> **For if you forgive men for their transgressions, your heavenly Father will also forgive you.**
> **But if you do not forgive men, then your Father will not forgive your transgressions (Matthew 6:14-15).**

This is by no means intended to imply that we can compromise the biblical standards for integrity in ministry. Until we learn to restore our fallen brethren, even those who are caught in "any trespass," the gates of hell will remain open against the church in the same areas where the enemy was able to cause these brethren to fall. As we work to restore them to the biblical stature of integrity required for ministry, we will gain great wisdom and knowledge as to the way that the enemy is gaining access to the church. Our eyes will also be opened to many of our own weaknesses. This is essential before the Lord can trust us with the anointing required for the end time ministry.

CHAPTER SIX

The Message

"**The testimony of Jesus is the spirit of prophecy**" (**Revelation 19:10** KJV). *Jesus is the prophetic message*; He is the Word of God. Christlikeness is the goal of every prophetic word. For Jesus to be our message, He must first be in our hearts, not just our minds. True Living Water can only come out of "the innermost being," the heart and not the mind. Only when Jesus is the passion of our hearts will we have the true Spirit of Prophecy. The apostle Paul explained that it was after the Father revealed His Son *in him*, not just *to him,* that he preached (see Galatians 1:15-16 KJV).

Ezekiel was told to first **"eat the scroll"** before he could speak to the house of Israel (see Ezekiel 3:1-4). The prophet was required to digest the message himself before he was free to share it with others. Until the message is a part of us, until it has been absorbed into our own lives, it will not be the true testimony or come with the power and authority of the true prophetic word.

Paul told Timothy to pay attention to his own teachings, because most of what we are hearing is for us first. What we feel compelled to preach the most is usually what the Lord is trying to say to us. This does not mean that it is wrong to preach it; but it is, if we are not living it ourselves.

The False Hope

I have watched many have to leave the ministry because of failure, as I myself once did. I did not leave because of a moral or ethical failure, but the failure of my ministry. I could not accomplish what I felt called to accomplish. This type of failure is usually accompanied by a great frustration with the church, or with people in general. That in itself should be a revelation of how misplaced our faith and vision are.

We are not called to build the church—Jesus is going to build His church, and it will be all that He desires for it to be. We can partake of that only to the degree that we abide in Him. If there is no fruit, it should tell us more about where we are spiritually than where the people are. We will only be frustrated with the people if our hope has been wrongly placed in them.

The Lord Himself is the example of true ministry. He did not do what He saw men doing. He only did what He saw the Father doing. When we observe the way that He led and prepared His leaders, it is a shock to our human reasoning. It seems that He did not know anything about good management principles! Yet, somehow, He upholds all things by the word of His power. Maybe there is a higher way to build the church than we can learn from business!

When just one of the Lord's disciples received the revelation of Who He was, He identified it as enough to build His church on—it was now time for Him to go to the cross and leave them. Then, when He needed their faithfulness the most, all but one scattered, betraying and denying Him. Yet, He had every confidence that His church would not only survive, but ultimately prevail against the gates of hell. How could He have such confidence? Because His confidence was not in men, even the men who he had chosen and trained, but His hope was in the Holy Spirit. When our hope is rightly placed on the Lord, we will not be overly discouraged when men fail us, or overly encouraged when they do well.

The finished work of God has already been accomplished, which is Jesus Christ Himself. All that we are called to do is abide in Him, and point others to Him. When we, like Abraham, see the Lamb that God has provided, we can easily sacrifice even His own promises to us in this temporary realm, knowing that they are forever reserved for us in eternity.

Frustration with the people is a sign that *we* have seriously diverted from the path, and from the true faith that is the source of true spiritual authority. If we are frustrated, we will only minister frustration, and the frustrations that we sow in the people will be returned on our own heads. True faith walks and believes in what Jesus has already accomplished, and will not be discouraged by the appearances of the temporary realm. If we have faith in Jesus, we will impart faith in Him, and eventually those seeds will sprout and bear fruit.

Be patient, therefore, brethren, until the coming of the Lord. Behold, the farmer waits for the precious produce of the soil, being patient about it, until it gets the early and late rains.

You too be patient; strengthen your hearts, for the coming of the Lord is at hand.

Do not complain, brethren, against one another, that you yourselves may not be judged; behold, the Judge is standing right at the door.

As an example, brethren, of suffering and patience, take the prophets who spoke in the name of the Lord.

Behold, we count those blessed who endured. You have heard of the endurance of Job and have seen the outcome of the Lord's dealings, that the Lord is full of compassion and *is* merciful (James 5:7-11).

The Proceeding Word

"We do not live by bread alone, but by every word which *proceeds* from the mouth of God" (Matthew 4:4 NKJV). This is not to indicate a word which proceeded, but the continuing, *proceeding* word. We must have this fresh manna everyday; yesterday's revelation cannot be stored or kept. Manna which was kept overnight for the next day spoiled. If we are to serve fresh bread, we must be gathering fresh bread each day. Jesus must be new to us each morning.

When Moses asked the Lord His name, He declared that He was "I Am"; not "I Was" or "I Will Be." If we are to know the true God, we must know Him today. It is not enough to know the historic Jesus or the Jesus who will return; we must partake of the God Who *IS*. It is good to know who He was and who He will be, but we cannot live by that knowledge; we can only live by the fresh encounter we have with Him each day. He must be our "daily Bread." Jesus is the Word which *proceeds* from the mouth of God by which we must live.

Because **"the testimony of Jesus is the spirit of prophecy,"** true ministry must be Christ-centered and not issue-centered. Jesus is not just *in* the message; He *IS* the prophetic message. The New Testament prophet is not given to just affect the behavior of the church; he is given to impart Christ to the church that she might abide in Him. Disciplines can change behavior, and they can be profitable, but only Christ can change hearts. Apostles and prophets are not given just to bring the church into a certain form, but to assist the forming of Christ within her.

Signs Are Messages

Every miracle of Jesus was a message. Signs are just that—*signs* that point us to God. In the sixth chapter of the Gospel of John, Jesus took the loaves and fishes and fed the multitude. This was an illustration of the heart of the multitude; they were partaking of many loaves, or truths, which could satisfy them for one meal, but only fragments were left over. When we are inclined to partake of individual emphases or truths, it will always lead to the fragmenting of the church, with each group thinking their little fragment is the whole truth.

Jesus corrected the inclination of the multitude, declaring that He was the Bread from heaven, the One Loaf. As a result of this "hard saying," many of His own disciples departed from Him (verse 66). This is still a primary point of demarcation for many who would be His disciples. It is sometimes easier to be loyal to a truth than it is to submit to *the* Truth, Himself. It is not hearing the words of the Lord that matters; it is hearing the Word, Himself.

True Christianity is not just belief in truths and compliance with doctrines or disciplines; it is a relationship with God. Only when we are partaking of the one Loaf can we serve the one Loaf, and only then will our message cease to just fragment the body of Christ. As the writer of Hebrews explained, **"God, after He spoke long ago to the fathers by the prophets in many portions and in many ways, in these last days has spoken to us *in His Son"* (Hebrews 1:1-2).** The message of God no longer comes in words but in the Word, the Son of God Himself. Jesus did not come to give us new truths; He came to be the Truth.

Does this mean that we no longer have prophetic messages or revelations? Of course not. As Peter explained in his message on the day of Pentecost, when the Lord pours out His Spirit there will be prophecy, dreams and visions, accompanied by signs in the heavens and on the earth (see Acts 2:17-21). The issue is not whether there will be prophecy but what is to be the content of the prophecy.

The church will probably never become the church she is called to be as long as that is her primary focus. The church is not the pattern for the church—Jesus is the Pattern for the church. We will not be changed by looking at ourselves, but by staying focused on the glory of the Lord. When we can forget who we are and focus on who He is, we will be changed into who we are called to be.

The job of ministry is first and foremost to impart a vision for true worship of the Lord. True worship does not come in order to see the Lord, but from seeing Him. This does not mean that we should not try to see Him more in worship, but we are not looking *for* Him so much as we are looking *at* Him. One of the whole purposes of worship is to help us keep our attention focused upon the Lord. In fact, we are worshipping with our lives that which holds most of our attention. True worship should, therefore, be an increasing focus of our vision upon the Lord.

That is why it is seldom good to encourage churches, or ministries, to simply become models for others. That will only have them focus on themselves, and others, rather than the One who is the model for us all. Some are called to be models for others, and Christians are called to be models for the world. That is what it means to be "the light of the world." However, the way we will become that light is by being conformed to His image, which can only come through Christ-centeredness, not self-centeredness. To focus on being a model can give short term inspiration, but it will be short lived, and can, in fact, become a stumbling block to those for whom we are modeling.

It is only when the entire focus of our attention is upon seeing the Son of God receive the glory that is due Him and the reward of His sacrifice, that we can be trusted with true spiritual authority. It is only when our vision is single upon the Son of God that we will be full of light. To even be concerned about our own reward or glory is a sure indication that we have not yet truly perceived the sacrifice of the Lamb of God. When the Lamb enters, even the twenty-four elders cast their crowns at His feet. Who could presume glory or position in His presence?

New Covenant Prophecy and Teaching

The prophets were given to Israel to keep the people focused upon the worship of the one true God, and to bring correction when they drifted into idolatry. New Testament prophecy does have a similar function, but this gift was never given to establish doctrines, but rather to point to the person of Jesus. Many of the most destructive heresies of the New Testament Age have had their origin in a prophecy, vision, dream or revelation which emphasized *a* truth instead of *the* Truth, Jesus.

We should beware of any so called prophetic message which testifies of a specific doctrine, emphasis, or minister other than Christ Jesus Himself. The Lord does not use prophecy to establish doctrines, or to testify of men, but of Himself.

Doctrines are teachings and He uses teaching to establish them. The teaching ministry is the illumination of the Scriptures, not prophetic revelation. Some of the wonderfully gifted prophetic men in this century fell into serious error and died tragically deceived because they tried to become teachers and to establish new doctrines. Likewise, many of the most destructive false prophecies have come from gifted pastors or teachers who tried to be prophets.

The Source of False Ministry

Anyone will be false when attempting to function out of the sphere of his calling. Most false prophets were actually teachers who tried to assume a ministry God had not given to them. Likewise, many false teachers were prophets or evangelists who tried to teach beyond their level of grace. Every ministry is a sacred trust, and we cannot just take one upon ourselves.

There are actually more warnings in Scripture about false shepherds and false teachers than false prophets. Throughout the Scriptures and church history, shepherds and teachers have made greater mistakes and caused far more problems than prophets. Does this mean that we should throw out those ministries? Of course not. Neither can we throw out the prophetic ministry, but we should all have the wisdom to closely examine how these mistakes are made so that we will not be so prone to repeat them.

We need prophets and teachers in the church, and they need to be working together, with the shepherds, evangelists and apostles. However, we must beware when either starts trying to do the other's job. There is always some crossover. Prophets may help restore someone, and pastors may certainly prophesy, but when we begin to go beyond the sphere of authority that we have been given, tragedy will follow.

Motives and Spiritual Gifts

Paul exhorted the Corinthians to **"pursue love, yet desire earnestly spiritual gifts, but** *especially* **that you may prophesy" (I Corinthians 14:1).** Without love, discernment and revelation will become suspicion and criticism. The pursuit of love must supersede our desire for spiritual gifts, but we are commanded to *earnestly desire* the gifts, too, especially prophecy. This was a command, not a suggestion.

Just as some have their ministries perverted when self-seeking enters, many have their ministries aborted because of false guilt. These would pursue their gifts and callings, but they are thwarted because wrong motives sometimes arise in them, causing them to withdraw with feelings of unworthiness. It is a false teaching, rooted in a religious spirit, which projects that a believer must attain a certain level of perfection before God can use him. If this were the case, there would not have been a Pentecost and there would not be a church.

Some of the greatest acts of faith were performed by new believers. Most believers do the majority of the witnessing that they will do in their life, and lead almost all who they will lead to the Lord, in the first two years after their own conversion. After that, most Christians become too "mature" to witness and actually do very little for the rest of their lives. When we cease to witness it is not because of maturity—it is because of stagnation.

The Lord is not impressed with how long we have known Him, how many times we have read the Bible, or by how much we pray. It does not matter whether we have known the Lord for 20 years or 20 days; what matters to Him is if we are abiding in His Son. His Son came to save those who are lost. True spiritual maturity is a life that has not been beguiled from the simplicity of devotion to Christ, and His purposes.

God is in our heart by the Holy Spirit. It says that Satan accuses the saints before our God day and night (see Revelation 12:10). This speaks of the constant accusation that comes against the heart of every believer. This accuser must be replaced with the Redeemer. Our motives may be good one day and terrible the next. If we are going to be controlled by our motives, we will be continually perplexed and neutralized.

"The heart is more deceitful than all else . . . Who can understand it?" (Jeremiah 17:9). We must not be controlled by our own hearts, but by the Spirit of God and by His word. If we will first concentrate upon the will of God, regardless of what is going on in our hearts, we will soon find that our hearts have lined up with His will.

This also reveals the truth that the closer we get to the throne the more accusation we can expect. This could not be done if God did not allow it. He allows it, because learning to overcome accusations and rejection helps us to identify with the One who suffered the worst accusation and rejection, and prepares us to handle the authority that comes with being close to His throne.

When the Lord commissioned Moses at the burning bush, he claimed to be unworthy and inadequate. We may think that he was being humble, but it was a false humility that masked a terrible arrogance. By this, Moses was actually declaring that his inadequacy was greater than God's adequacy. Because of this, the anger of the Lord burned against him.

Moses *was* inadequate; so are you and I, and we always will be! Our righteousness, or adequacy, will never gain us favor or enable us to come boldly before the Throne of Grace. The blood of Jesus, *alone,* can do this, and it is by grace alone that we will accomplish the will of God. We are simply determining whether or not we will receive His grace so as to be used by Him.

He chooses the weak, foolish and base things of this world to confound the wise and strong (see I Corinthians 1:27). That is why, when we are weak and foolish young Christians, that He tends to use us more than when we become "mature and wise." He chose us because we were either weak, foolish or base, or all three. He did not call us for our strengths but for our weaknesses, so that His strength could be made perfect in us.

If we are going to be a prophetic people, self-righteousness and presumption must be removed in both of its forms—pride and self-assurance, or false humility. Jesus is our righteousness, and He is the work the Father seeks to do in us and through us.

It is only when we focus on ourselves, and try to make a name or ministry for ourselves, that we become self-conscious to the point where we will not do anything until we are sure we are right. At this point, we are crippled because we even prophesy according to our faith. **"Faith is the substance of things hoped for, the evidence of things not seen" (Hebrews 11:1 KJV).**

We may claim that we do not want to make a mistake because we do not want to hurt anyone, but the Lord and everyone else knows that the real reason is that we do not want to look foolish—which is pride. If we really believe that God gives His grace to the humble we should not mind being made to look small. Trying to protect our self-image probably keeps us from seeing more of the power and glory of God than anything else.

CHAPTER SEVEN

Words of Life

Death and life are in the power of the tongue, and those who love it will eat its fruit (Proverbs 18:21).

Words can have a most extraordinary power. In a basic way, the definition of life might be *communication*. To communicate basically means "to exchange," or have interchange. We determine that something is alive as long as it is able to communicate, or interrelate, with its environment—to breathe the air, partake of food, etc. When this exchange stops, death has come. We call an entity a higher form of life that can communicate on a higher level. Jesus said, **"The words that I have spoken to you are *spirit and are life"* (John 6:63).**

We have true spiritual life to the degree that our communication with the Lord is developed and maintained. If we have spiritual communication with Jesus, they can kill the body but they cannot kill us, because our lives are on a higher level. Our lives are hidden with God in Christ.

Jesus is the Word of God. He is the Father's communication with the creation. Those who hear His voice are joined to the greatest power in the universe, and it is a power of life. One word from the Lord and the creation was formed. The Lord did not think and bring forth the creation—He spoke and it came forth. The Lord did not say, "Think and this mountain will be moved," but, "*Speak* to the mountain . . ." (see Matthew 17:20). Words are the conduit for the greatest power there is—the power of God. The more spiritual we become, the more we will understand this.

Words Are Treasures

As we become more closely joined to the Word Himself, the more precious and powerful our words will become. As I heard one preacher say, it is amazing how few words the Word Himself used. The more valuable a thing is to us, the more careful we will be in handling it. As we comprehend the power and value of words, the more careful we will be with them. The more careful that we are with this great power, the more power the Lord can trust us with.

Like apples of gold in settings of silver is a word spoken in right circumstances (Proverbs 25:11).

Words spoken in right circumstances fit perfectly. Words that are spoken out of time can lose their power. *The anointing is connected to timing.* The Lord moves in perfect order and perfect timing, and if we are going to be used to speak His words we must be sensitive to His timing.

The Lord's whole life on this earth was a testimony to the grace of timing. It was timing that gave His teaching such penetrating power. He knew exactly when and what to say in every circumstance. He used the woman at the well to bring out His message on living waters. He knew that the teaching on being born again would seize the attention of Nicodemus, who was getting old. Had those teachings been given in the opposite settings they would probably not have had the impact that they did.

In this same way, what the Lord anoints for one person or group may not be what He anoints for another. The seven churches in Revelation, even though they all lived at the same time and in the same geographic location, each needed a different word.

In an exposition of the importance of knowing the language of the Spirit, Paul said:

Yet we do speak wisdom among those who are mature; a wisdom, however, not of this age, nor of the rulers of this age, who are passing away;

but we speak God's wisdom in a mystery, the hidden wisdom, which God predestined before the ages to our glory;

the wisdom which none of the rulers of this age has understood; for if they had understood it, they would not have crucified the Lord of glory;

but just as it is written, "Things which eye has not seen and ear has not heard, and which have not entered the heart of man, all that God has prepared for those who love Him."

For to us God revealed them through the Spirit; for the Spirit searches all things, even the depths of God.

For who among men knows the thoughts of a man except the spirit of the man, which is in him? Even so the thoughts of God no one knows except the Spirit of God.

Now we have received, not the spirit of the world, but the Spirit who is from God, that we might know the things freely given to us by God,

which things we also speak, not in words taught by human wisdom, but in those taught by the Spirit, *combining spiritual thoughts with spiritual words.*

But a natural man does not accept the things of the Spirit of God; for they are foolishness to him, and he cannot understand them, because they are spiritually appraised.

But he who is spiritual appraises all things, yet he himself is appraised by no man.

For who has known the mind of the Lord, that he should instruct Him? But we have the mind of Christ (I Corinthians 2:6-16).

There is a language of the Spirit that transcends human language. It is contrary and offensive to the natural mind of men. This is one reason why the Lord has spoken to men through dreams and visions from the beginning. He is not trying to confuse us by all of the strange symbols and metaphors in dreams and visions, but He is trying to teach us the language of the Spirit, which is much greater than human language.

It has been said that "a picture is worth a thousand words." In the language of the Spirit this is true. The symbolism of dreams and visions often reveal far more than human language can. This is foolishness to the natural mind, but for those who are spiritual, it is a much higher form of communication.

The primary difference between the languages of men and the language of the Spirit is that the former comes from the mind and the latter comes from the heart. Living waters come from the "innermost being." To share that which will be true life we must share that which comes from our hearts, not just our minds.

Christus *In* You

The Jewish exorcists in Acts 19:13-16 knew about Jesus, but He did not dwell in their hearts. Therefore, when they tried to use His name to drive out darkness, the darkness rose up and drove them out. Demons are spiritual creatures, and they only respond to words that are spirit. For our words to have the power of light to drive out darkness, they must come from our innermost being, because Christ dwells in our hearts, and we only have true spiritual authority to the degree that the King dwells within us.

This does not mean that we cannot ever share that which was first given to someone else. Every time we share from the Scriptures we do that. But the words must become "ours." We cannot have a relationship through another person's knowledge of Jesus—He must be our Jesus. True ministry is not just parroting knowledge. True ministry is by the Spirit; and only the Spirit can beget that which is spiritual.

And as for you, the anointing which you received from Him abides in you, and you have no need for anyone to teach you; but as His anointing teaches you about all things, and is true and is not a lie, and just as it has taught you, you abide in Him (I John 2:27).

This does not mean that we do not receive teaching from men, as the Lord gave teachers to His church for that reason, but we must recognize the anointing of the Holy Spirit working through these men. The men on the road to Emmaus were sensitive to the spiritual words spoken to them by Jesus because their hearts burned within them. However, they did not recognize the Lord until they saw Him break the bread. It is when we see Jesus as the one who is breaking our bread, Jesus as our Teacher, regardless of the earthly vessel, that our eyes, too, will begin to open.

The Power of Truth

Charles Spurgeon once lamented that he could find ten men who would die for the Bible for every one who would read it. This ratio is probably still accurate today, and for our other Christian duties as well. We can probably find ten men who will fight for prayer in public schools for every one who actually prays with his own children at home. We may have ten men and women who complain about the sex and violence on television for every one who actually refuses to watch it. This must and will change. Our power to be salt and light in the world does not depend just on what we believe, but on our faithfulness to our beliefs.

"That which is born of the flesh is flesh; and that which is born of the Spirit is spirit" (John 3:6 KJV). We are utterly dependent on the Holy Spirit for bearing spiritual fruit. Because the Holy Spirit is "the Spirit of truth," He will only endorse with His presence and power that which is true. The Lord judges our hearts, not our minds. For this reason, "heart religion" is about to take precedence over intellectual religion. However, we must never abandon our commitment to sound biblical doctrine. The highest levels of power will be to those who have embraced both the Word and the Spirit.

The great darkness that is now sweeping the world has happened on our watch. The coming great release of power in Christian leadership will be the result of a great repentance and conviction of sin sweeping over the body of Christ. Movements that exhort men and women to faithfulness and their spiritual responsibilities will have a profound impact on the whole church. The repentance that resulted from the humiliations of the last years are also about to bear great fruit.

The Lord declared, **"Whoever exalts himself shall be humbled; and whoever humbles himself shall be exalted" (Matthew 23:12).** Even though much of the humility has been the result of judgment, the degree to which the church embraced the judgment has prepared her to be lifted up in the esteem of the nations. Even though the attacks and slander will always be with us, the world's esteem for the advancing church is about to rise.

Only Patience Bears Lasting Fruit

Some consider it a travesty that the New Testament does not take a decisive stand against some of the greatest moral evils of the times in which it was written, such as slavery, abortion and infanticide (the practice of killing babies if they were not the desired sex, or had defects). It is true that the first century leaders of the church did not begin frontal assaults against these great evils. However, it was not because of negligence or irresponsibility—they had a higher strategy and a greater power than such confrontation. They did not just flail at the branches of human depravity—they put the ax to the root of the tree.

With focused, unyielding concentration, the apostles to the early church maintained their frontal assault on sin. They drove back the spirit of death by lifting up the Prince of Life. When the issue of slavery did arise in his letter to Philemon, Paul did not attack the issue of slavery directly, but rose above it by appealing to love and the fact that Onesimus was a brother.

This tactic may offend the penchant for militancy that issue-oriented activists usually have, but it is the way of the Spirit. The secular historian Will Durant understood it, saying, "Caesar tried to change men by changing institutions. Christ changed institutions by changing men."

The way of the Spirit is to penetrate beyond what a frontal assault on issues can usually accomplish. There are times for bold confrontations, but usually the Lord works much more slowly than we are willing to accept. This is because He is working toward a much deeper, more complete change—working from the inside out, not the outside in.

We Have a Higher Power

The divinely powerful weapons are about to be reclaimed and used on an unprecedented scale by the church. As intercessory and spiritual warfare movements continue to mature, the results will become increasingly spectacular. Even so, the most powerful weapon given to the church is *spiritual truth.*

Facts can be "truth," but spiritual truth is only found when knowledge is properly combined with life. It is when we live what we believe that we embrace spiritual, eternal truth. As the church begins to live the truth that she knows, her light will increase and shine into the darkness.

Light is more powerful than darkness. Love is more powerful than hatred. Life is more powerful than death. As we begin to walk in the light, love and life of the Son of God, we will put darkness and death to flight. The power of the church does not lie in her ability to just articulate the truth, but to walk in it. This is the foundation of the great release of power coming to the church.

The Greater Wisdom

The way of the Spirit is practical. He does want the will of God to be done on earth as it is in heaven. We, too, must be committed to seeing practical fruit. However, our desire not to be so heavenly minded that we do not do any earthly good has often resulted in our becoming so earthly minded that we are not doing any spiritual good. If we impact men spiritually it will ultimately result in earthly good, but the reverse is not true. If we only impact institutions and outward behavior, we may change the facade of things, but we have not dealt with the roots and they will sprout again.

It is not just bearing fruit that counts, but bearing fruit that remains. For us to bear the fruit that is eternal we must learn patience. The great wisdom that is about to come upon the church is to see first from the eternal perspective, which will impart the essential ability to plan with strategy and vision for lasting fruit on earth.

CHAPTER EIGHT

Our Ministry as Priests

One of the great truths that was recovered by the Reformation is the priesthood of all believers. This is a doctrine that almost all Protestants and Evangelicals now believe. However, that which is so generally believed is often generally overlooked, and seldom implemented. Tragically, this has been the case with this great truth about our priestly ministry.

What does it really mean to be a priest of the Most High God? This subject is so profound and expansive that it is not possible to fully answer it in a single chapter, but it is important that we review the fundamentals of this crucial issue. Few things can so change our lives, the church, and the world in general, as when the church begins to live this truth.

The Foundation of All Ministry

What is a priest? This term was generally understood by both the Jews and pagans during the first century. The early Christians derived their understanding from the Old Covenant type, which was at that time still performing in the temple in Jerusalem. But the modern evangelical church does not have this advantage. In general, little attention has been given to understanding this ministry that is supposed to be a basic function for all New Covenant believers.

When the institutional church tried to implement these truths, it did what is natural for an institution to do—it institutionalized them. This actually separated these truths from the lives of all but a few professionals. The Reformation did recover the truth that this was a ministry to which all believers are called. Even so, the recovery of the practical application of this truth has still made little progress in the actual life of the church. Where progress has been made, its effect has been so extraordinary that we fill our church libraries with the books written about the revivals and moves of God that were the result. We view these as exceptional acts of grace, but they are supposed to be normal church life.

The life and power that the first century church experienced is meant to be normal Christianity. Without question, the power and life that they experienced, and all who have moved in the great grace of God since, have been the result of believers beginning to *live* by the basic truth that we are all called as priests. This truth of the priesthood of all believers is a foundation of all ministry, and to the degree that it is neglected, our foundation has been weakened.

Under the Old Covenant, the priest was the primary spiritual mediator between God and men. He was not the only mediator, because the Lord raised up prophets as spokesmen, and He was represented in civil matters by the kings and elders. The priests were commissioned to mediate for the people with regard to their relationship to the Lord, and the civil authority was commissioned to mediate for the people in their civil relations with each other.

Because the function of Old Covenant priests was to a great degree devoted to the offering of sacrifices and the performing of rituals required by the Law, it is understandable that the institutional church would succumb to such a high degree of ritual in the development of its priestly offices. It makes sense that these functions were delegated to a special class of professionals. The Old Covenant type was a separate tribe, the Levites, who were designated specifically for this function, with a very strict ban disallowing anyone from the other tribes to perform these duties. However, to understand the types properly, we must first understand that with the change of covenants, the Lord profoundly changed the rules by which men are allowed to approach Him.

For there is one God, and one mediator also between God and men, the man Christ Jesus (I Timothy 2:5 kjv).

Jesus is now the only mediator between God and men. We partake of this ministry only as we abide in Him. Our goal for this ministry is to introduce others to Him, and to help them to so connect to Him that they no longer need us. Even so, this is not our main function as priests. Our main function is to minister to the Lord.

Now when these things have been thus prepared, the priests are continually entering the outer tabernacle, performing the divine worship (Hebrews 9:6).

The ministry in the Outer Court was to the people, but the ministry in the tabernacle was to the Lord. Here we see that the priests were "continually entering" the tabernacle to perform this divine worship, or ministry to Him. Much of what we consider ministry, what we usually devote most of our time to in ministry is the Outer Court ministry to the people. This is the reverse of what we should be doing in ministry.

The Foundation of the Priestly Ministry

The first responsibility of all in ministry is to minister to the Lord, not to men. The ministry that we have to men should be the result of our ministry to the Lord. All true spiritual fruit will come as the result of our union with Him. When we give ourselves to the Lord first, we will have much more to give the people. The anointing comes from the presence of the Lord. We can have the best messages ever preached, but have no true spiritual fruit if the Holy Spirit does not endorse it with His anointing.

And as for you, the anointing which you received from Him abides in you, and you have no need for anyone to teach you; but as His anointing teaches you

about all things, and is true and is not a lie, and just as it has taught you, you abide in Him (I John 2:27).

This is not saying that we do not need teachers, for they were given by the Lord to the church for the equipping of His people. However, teaching without the anointing does not profit us spiritually. The purpose of all ministry is to draw men closer to the Lord, that we may more fully abide in Him. The Holy Spirit was given to testify of Jesus, and the Spirit does not anoint teaching or preaching which has not originated with Jesus or which does not draw men to Him.

For example, we can teach our people about unity so that they understand every aspect of the doctrine, but that does not necessarily unify them. Let the right circumstances come along and there will be a great division if the knowledge that they have in their minds has not been transferred to their hearts. **"For with the *heart* [not the mind] man believes, resulting in righteousness" (Romans 10:10).** Knowledge without the anointing may stimulate our minds, and we may intellectually agree with it, but we will only live it if it has been transferred to our hearts by the Holy Spirit. We receive the anointing from being in the presence of the Lord.

Light Brings Unity

Upon entering the first compartment of the tabernacle there was a golden lampstand on the left, which burned olive oil for light, representing the Holy Spirit. The table of shewbread was on the right, and at the far end was the altar of incense. The table of shewbread had twelve loaves of bread symbolizing the twelve tribes of Israel. They were set in two rows to symbolize their unity (in Scripture the number two often symbolizes unity, i.e., "the two shall become one," see Genesis 2:24).

As a part of the service in the tabernacle, wine was poured as an oblation in front of the table. This made the table a prophecy of communion, or the common-union of God's people in Jesus. The loaves were in unity to represent this communion, being placed directly across from the lampstand, and continually bathed in the light of the Holy Spirit, or the anointing. As the apostle John wrote:

> **but if we walk in the light as He Himself is in the light, we have fellowship [Greek *koinonea*, "communion"] with one another, and the blood of Jesus His Son cleanses us from all sin (I John 1:7).**

True unity comes from abiding in the light with the Son of God, together. Anything less will be superficial at best. Those who abide in the light would not be prone to do things that create division. Our job as priests is not to just go out to tell the people about the Light in the Holy Place, but to lead the people into that Light. In Christ all are called to be priests, and all must learn to "continually enter" His presence to perform the divine service. Those who do not learn to abide in that place will not stay unified, regardless of how much we talk about it.

> **But *we all*, with an unveiled face beholding as in a mirror the glory of the Lord, are being transformed into the same image from glory to glory, just as from the Lord, the Spirit (II Corinthians 3:18).**

Teaching is important, but people are not changed just by knowing the doctrines—they must behold the glory of the Lord. A few minutes in the manifest presence of the Lord can accomplish more than many weeks, or even years, of teaching. Teaching that comes from the presence of the Lord, which is anointed by the Holy Spirit, will lead those who hear into His presence where the knowledge is transferred from the mind to the heart.

The Altar of Incense

The altar of incense that was also in the Holy Place represents prayer and intercession. David wrote, **"May my prayer be counted as incense before Thee; the lifting up of my hands as the evening offering" (Psalm 141:2; also see Revelation 8:4).** The Lord said that His house was to be **"a

house of prayer for all nations" (Isaiah 56:7 NIV). This specifies prayer for all people as a major purpose for the house in which He has chosen to dwell. Never did He say that His house would be a house of preaching, a house of healing, or even a house of fellowship. Certainly all of these are found in His house, but He obviously meant for prayer to be foremost. Therefore, if we are to be His dwelling place, prayer should be our highest priority.

How can we dwell continually in the presence of the Lord to perform the divine service? When the building of the altar of incense was first commissioned, the Lord offered us a type.

> **And Aaron shall burn fragrant incense on it; he shall burn it every morning when he trims the lamps.**
> **And when Aaron trims the lamps at twilight, he shall burn incense.** *There shall be perpetual incense before the Lord throughout your generations* **(Exodus 30:7-8).**

Aaron was to light the incense as his first duty each morning, and as the last thing he did at night, but there would be "perpetual incense before the Lord." This was a statement that if we will learn to begin our days with prayer, and then end them in prayer, we will be able to stay in a perpetual attitude of prayer, knowing His presence continually. The Lord does not just want us to talk to Him a couple of times a day; He wants us to abide in Him.

If we really are His temple, and His Spirit abides in us, how is it that we ignore Him so much? The Lord wants to have fellowship with us in everything we do. How much would our typical day change if the Lord appeared in the flesh, and went with us everywhere that day? The truth is that if the eyes of our hearts were opened we would see Him in all that we do, and the reality of His presence would actually be greater than that which we are seeing with our physical eyes. Then we would also manifest the sweet aroma of the knowledge of Him in every place, as we are called to do as His dwelling place.

As Paul explained, **"Now these things [the experiences of Israel in the wilderness] happened to them as an example, and they were written for our instruction, upon whom the ends of the ages have come" (I Corinthians 10:11).** The Lord does not want literal incense rising to Him, as he explained later through the prophets, but He does want our prayers.

Instead of "thinking to ourselves," He wants us to be conversing with Him. **"We are destroying speculations and every lofty thing raised up against the knowledge of God, and we are taking every thought captive to the obedience of Christ" (II Corinthians 10:5).** If we take the time to properly light this fire the first thing in the morning, and then as the last thing we do at night, soon we will find ourselves raising perpetual prayer as incense before the Lord, coming from our hearts.

The Place of Sacrifice

The temple was from beginning to end a place of sacrifice. The altar of burnt offering where the sacrifices were made graced the entrance of the Outer Court. The priests who served there were usually covered in blood and guts. It was not a pretty sight, just as the cross was not the pretty stained glass window scene we have often portrayed it as.

The cross was one of the most perverted and cruel exhibitions of the demented human mind. The Lord is not just trying to change us—He's trying to kill us! True Christianity requires the ultimate price—the "whole burnt offering," which means our whole life must be placed on the altar.

The fire on the Altar of Incense was originally lit from the fire on the Altar of Burnt Offerings, which typified the cross. It does require sacrifice to pray. We must give up our self-life. The Lord is not just after a few minutes of our day—He wants every thought taken captive and brought into obedience to Him.

Modern Western Christianity is different from the Christianity found throughout the rest of the world, or its biblical counterpart. More than any other place or time, Western Christianity is in the stranglehold of the Laodicean spirit of lukewarmness. If we are going to fulfill our calling for these times we must embrace the reality of that which we have been proclaiming for the last five hundred years—we must all begin to walk in our calling to the priestly ministry. It is a difficult place, and it will require the sacrifice, but this is the purpose for which we were apprehended by the Lord, and we must now answer the call.

For the love of Christ controls us, having concluded this, that one died for all, therefore all died;

and He died for all, *that they who live should no longer live for themselves,* **but for Him who died and rose again on their behalf (II Corinthians 5:14-15).**

We are called to give Him "the sacrifice of praise," etc. There is a reason why the Altar of Incense is called an "altar"; it is a place of sacrifice and death. It requires sacrifice to perform our duties properly in ministry to the people. Our ministry as priests is founded upon sacrifice, and our effectiveness will be determined by the degree of our sacrifice, as we see in the following texts:

For just as the sufferings of Christ are ours in abundance, so also our comfort is abundant through Christ.

But if we are afflicted, it is for your comfort and salvation; or if we are comforted, it is for your comfort, which is effective in the patient enduring of the same sufferings which we also suffer;

and our hope for you is firmly grounded, knowing that as you are sharers of our sufferings, so also you are sharers of our comfort.

For we do not want you to be unaware, brethren, of our affliction which came to us in Asia, that we were burdened excessively, beyond our strength, so that we despaired even of life;

indeed we had the sentence of death within ourselves in order that we should not trust in ourselves, but in God who raises the dead (II Corinthians 1:5-9).

But we have this treasure in earthen vessels, that the surpassing greatness of the power may be of God and not from ourselves;

we are afflicted in every way, but not crushed; perplexed, but not despairing;

persecuted, but not forsaken; struck down, but not destroyed;

always carrying about in the body the dying of Jesus, that the life of Jesus also may be manifested in our body.

For we who live are constantly being delivered over to death for Jesus' sake, that the life of Jesus also may be manifested in our mortal flesh (II Corinthians 4:7-11).

For the love of Christ controls us, having concluded this, that one died for all, therefore all died;

and He died for all, that they who live should no longer live for themselves, but for Him who died and rose again on their behalf (II Corinthians 5:14-15).

For to you it has been granted for Christ's sake, not only to believe in Him, but also to suffer for His sake (Philippians 1:29).

and if children, heirs also, heirs of God and fellow heirs with Christ, if indeed we suffer with Him in order that we may also be glorified with Him (Romans 8:17).

Therefore, since Christ has suffered in the flesh, arm yourselves also with the same purpose, because he who has suffered in the flesh has ceased from sin (I Peter 4:1).

The apostle Paul is one of the great examples of the New Covenant ministry. He died daily. He did all things for the sake of the gospel. He sacrificed his own will, safety, and comfort to serve the Lord and his people. Paul's great effectiveness in ministry can be directly tied to the degree to which he laid down his life for the purposes of the Lord.

There is power in sacrifice. The cross was the ultimate sacrifice and it is the ultimate power. The degree to which we will take up the cross daily will be the degree to which we experience the power of God in our daily lives. The priesthood is for intercession. Intercession is not prayer for yourself, but for others. The priesthood to which we are called is to live not for ourselves, but for others.

The ministry of intercession is the foundation of all ministry. Ministry is not living for ourselves but for others. Intercession is not just praying for ourselves but for others. The church is itself called to be a prophetic voice to the world, and we see this relationship between the prophetic ministry and intercession in Isaiah 62:6-7:

On your walls, O Jerusalem, I have appointed watchmen; all day and all night they will never keep silent. You who remind the LORD, take no rest for yourselves;

And give Him no rest until He establishes and makes Jerusalem a praise in the earth.

In I Samuel 12:23, the prophet declared: **"Moreover, as for me, far be it from me that I should sin against the Lord by ceasing to pray for you."** It would have been a sin against the Lord for the prophet to stop praying for the people, even though the people had just rejected the Lord by seeking a king for themselves. It is true that **"where your treasure is, there your heart will be also" (Matthew 6:21).** If we have an investment of prayer and intercession in people we are much more likely to have a right heart toward them, and to be able to represent the Lord to them without bias.

Love, The Foundation of Authority

True spiritual authority is founded upon love. Jesus felt compassion for the sheep so He became their Shepherd—His ministry as Shepherd was founded upon His compassion. Jesus felt compassion for the people who lived in darkness, so He became their Teacher. His teaching ministry was founded upon His compassion.

The same is true with us. We will not have true spiritual authority with any group, city or nation that we do not love. This love will either be the fruit of intercession, or it will result in intercession, but either way it will be tied to intercession. If we love someone we will pray for them. If we don't love them, but start to invest in them with prayer, we will begin to love them, and the Lord can give us a true ministry for them.

Everyone in ministry will be falsely accused, slandered, rejected and betrayed. This will often tempt us to call fire down from heaven on our accusers, but the Lord commanded us to pray *for* them, not *against* them. As we faithfully pray for our enemies we will start to have an investment in them. Then we will start to love them because, "Where our treasure (investment) is, there will our heart be also."

Because love is the foundation of spiritual authority, as we begin to love our enemies we will gain spiritual authority in their lives. Just as the Lord turned the greatest injustice of all time, the cross, into a power that could redeem the whole world, injustice can provide our greatest opportunity to grow in true spiritual authority. That is why Paul pointed to the beatings and stonings that he had taken as evidence of his spiritual authority as an apostle.

Jesus, our High Priest, died for the very ones who cried, "Crucify Him!" So must we lay down our lives for the sake of even our enemies. Jesus did not come to condemn the world, because it was already condemned. He did not even condemn the world when it rejected Him. Jesus came to save the world, and we have been sent to proclaim that great mercy of God. This mercy is most powerfully proclaimed in the midst of persecution.

When we start to intercede for others, we make an investment in their lives. This investment becomes a treasure, and where our treasure is there will our hearts be also. We begin to love them, and as we do, we can become a vessel of spiritual authority that can speak prophetically into their lives. This is how intercession becomes the foundation of prophetic ministry, which is what Samuel understood.

I usually know when the Lord starts putting a country on my heart that He is about to send me there. It is only after I have love for a country that He starts to speak to me about it. Even if the Lord gives me words of impending judgment for a country, I must have love for it before I can give those words. Anything but divine love will pervert our message. That is why He made Jeremiah love Israel so much that he would weep over her, even as he was foretelling her destruction.

A Costly Presumption

Moses was denied the blessing of leading the people into their Promised Land because the Lord told him to speak to the rock to bring forth water, but he struck the rock in anger. As a prophet he represented the Lord as angry when He was not, and it cost him dearly.

Many in ministry have likewise disqualified themselves from entering into their promises by mis-representing the Lord in this same way. One of the devastating dangers occurs when prophetic people think that, because the Lord speaks through us occasionally, He is just like we are, and that His feelings are our feelings. We must always attempt to distinguish our own feelings from that which is coming by the anointing.

"God is love," and we will only see as He sees when we love those we are beholding. Anything but love will distort our vision. I have learned never to trust "revelations" that come to me about those by whom I may have been rejected, while I still feel the pain of it.

Whenever I am rejected or attacked by others, they go on my prayer list. I pray for them and their ministry until I have such an investment in them that I must love them. In a sense this is selfish because it is for my sake as much as theirs. If bitterness gets a root in us it will defile us and many more. Whenever someone approaches me with a word of correction or judgment for another ministry, etc., I always ask if he loves that person or ministry, and how much prayer has gone forth on their behalf.

Therefore He is also able to save to the uttermost those who come to God through Him, since He always lives to make intercession for them (Hebrews 7:25 NKJV).

Jesus did not condemn the world when He saw its sin; He laid down His life for it. All who have a true ministry will do the same. Jesus died for the very ones who rejected Him. We, too, can be given authority to help save those who reject us if we will intercede for them, as He gave us an example, **"He is able to save to the uttermost . . . *since* He always lives to make intercession for them."**

Before He could save them, the Lord had to be rejected and persecuted by the ones He came to save. The same is often true for those who are called to any ministry. When we handle rejection properly it can open a wide door for effective ministry. We **"overcome evil with good" (Romans 12:21 KJV).**

We cannot overcome the evil until we have a confrontation with it. When we maintain the fruit of the Spirit in the face of evil we open the door for effective ministry. This is one reason why Paul suffered so much persecution, and he counted it as so valuable—persecution opens the door for ministry. That is why we must remain faithful to love our enemies.

The Main Thing

One of Peter Lord's famous sayings is, "The main thing is to keep the main thing the main thing." The first great commandment is to love the Lord. The second is to love our neighbors. If we reverse these two commands, we will only end up making an idol out of human love. Just as the priesthood requires ministry to the Lord first, we must always guard ourselves against loving the people more than we love the Lord. This will pervert the ministry.

The only way that we can keep the proper balance of loving the people, but representing the Lord first to the people, is by loving Him more than we love them. If we love the Lord more than we love the people we will end up loving them much more than we would otherwise. We will also have much more power with which to help them.

Elijah prayed for the judgments of the Lord to come on the people, but it was not out of his own wrath. God's wrath is not like man's wrath. Neither is His jealousy like man's, which is self-centered. We must always be careful not to represent our anger as being the Lord's, or we can end up like Moses and never experience the fullness of our calling. Likewise, we must never esteem the people above the Lord, or our whole ministry will be corrupted.

CHAPTER NINE

Wisdom for Building

Intimacy with God should be our highest goal. This is the Father's own desire for us. He loved us so much that He sent His only Son to pay a terrible price so we could come boldly before His throne. This is certainly the greatest privilege in all of creation—to have such access to the Most High God. The angels even marvel at the Lord's special affinity for man. However, there is an unholy familiarity with God that some fall into which can be a most deadly trap. Judas was familiar with Jesus, but John was intimate. There is a difference.

One who is in this precarious condition of an unholy familiarity will usually reject this kind of exhortation because it engenders in them an uncomfortable fear. However, the Scriptures are clear that if we do not have the proper fear of God we will depart from the path of life. It may well be that the lack of a pure and holy fear of God is one of the greatest causes of the unholy behavior in much of the modern church today. **"And by the fear of the LORD one keeps away from evil"** (Prov-erbs 16:6). **"How blessed is the man who fears [God] always, but he who hardens his heart will fall into calamity"** (Proverbs 28:14).

One of the Bible's most scathing denunciations of the con-dition of mankind, Romans 3:10-18, which is a compilation of quotes from the Old Testament, concludes with the reason for this great corruption: **"There is no fear of God before their eyes"** (verse 18). Jeremiah equated not having the fear of the Lord with forsaking the Lord: **" 'Your own wickedness will correct you, and your apostasies will reprove you; know therefore and see that it is evil and bitter for you to forsake the LORD your God, and the dread of Me is not in you,' declares the Lord GOD of hosts"** (Jeremiah 2:19).

There is a concept which many have that this fear is simply a reverence, or a respect, for God. Certainly that is implied, but we must understand that this is a reverence and respect to the highest degree. When either the Old or New Covenant saints encountered the living God, we would be hard pressed to call their reaction mere respect or reverence—they were so afraid that they were surprised that they lived through it!

John the Beloved was the Lord's very best friend; this friendship won him the privilege of leaning his head upon His breast, relaxing with the Lord in a wonderful picture of intimacy. Yet, near the end of a life spent in faithful service to Him, when he encountered the risen Lord, he fell to the ground **"as a dead man" (Revelation 1:17).** Anyone who does not have a true fear of the Lord has not seen Him as He is.

As the psalmist declared, **"The fear of the LORD is the beginning of wisdom" (Psalm 111:10 KJV).** Isaiah said, **"The fear of the LORD is his treasure" (Isaiah 33:6 KJV).** Proverbs 2:1-5 links these two great thoughts together in one of the great biblical exhortations:

> **My son, if you will receive my sayings, and treasure my commandments within you,**
> **Make your ear attentive to wisdom, incline your heart to understanding;**
> **For if you cry for discernment, lift your voice for understanding;**
> **If you seek her as silver, and search for her as for hidden treasures;**
> ***Then you will discern the fear of the LORD,* and discover the knowledge of God.**

Wisdom is a great treasure. Treasure is not found just laying on the ground, or growing on trees. What makes something a treasure is that it is either rare, or very hard to get to. Wisdom is such a treasure. It is hard to find and easy to lose. Even Solomon, the wisest man to walk the earth until Wisdom

Himself came, lost his wisdom and fell at the end of his life. When we find true wisdom we will find the fear of the Lord. When we lose the fear of the Lord we lose wisdom, regardless of how much knowledge or understanding we have.

It is understandable that there is so much confusion about the fear of the Lord. The true grace of the fear of the Lord is rare. Few are willing to pay the price to seek it, and it is something that we must seek. Wisdom will never come to those who do not seek it, and it will quickly be lost by all who do not genuinely value it. And the beginning of all wisdom is to properly fear the Lord.

If you knew for sure that there was a vein of gold in your backyard that could supply all of your needs for the rest of your life, you would be wise to quit your job and lay everything else aside to dig until you found it. However, there is treasure greater than the mother lode laying on many of our book-shelves, often just accumulating dust—the Bible!

Knowing the truth without living it only brings judgment. We may feel secure in our condition because we have had certain spiritual experiences, or attend church regularly, pay tithes, or submit ourselves to other spiritual disciplines, but the Lord repeatedly warned in His teachings that many who knew the truth, and even did great works, would not enter into the kingdom.

If we are like the foolish virgins and neglect to keep our vessels full of oil, when He comes we are going to be in a most desperate condition. Those foolish virgins were believers, who were waiting for Him to come. This may be a good time to check and see how much oil is in our own lamps!

One of the greatest treasures a man can possess is the true fear of the Lord. All of the other graces and blessings are protected by this grace. If we really have a heart to fear the Lord, we will spend our time seeking it. How many of us actually spend more time in front of the television each week, or even in the newspaper, than we do in our Bibles, or in prayer?

Many quit spending time in their Bibles, or in prayer, simply because it was so dry they did not feel that there was much profit in it. But that is almost certainly how it began for even the greatest Christian preachers. The difference is that they had such faith that the treasure was there that they did not quit digging until they found it. Treasure does not lie on the surface, and it will always be difficult to acquire. But who esteems it highly enough to give what it takes to find it? **"It is the glory of God to conceal a matter, but the glory of kings is to search out a matter" (Proverbs 25:2).**

Many of us, especially in the West, have been spoiled by an easy salvation. This is not to imply that we can do anything to attain salvation, but there are requirements for receiving it that are seldom preached in the West. For the first three centuries of the church, it usually required the sacrifice, or at least the risk of losing, everything that one possessed to become a Christian. At times this even included life itself.

After the church was institutionalized by the state, those who rejected the dogma of the state institutions of the church often suffered the same persecution, even to the present time in many countries. We should be very thankful for the religious liberty that we generally now have in the West, but it is very fragile. If we take it for granted it will almost certainly be lost. But even worse than that, if our salvation is taken for granted we can be in danger of losing it, regardless of how much religious liberty we have.

We have often preached both a salvation and a Christian life that reflects our addiction to convenience, which brings into question whether or not some of our concepts of salvation or the Christian life are even biblical. Tragically, many are being made to feel spiritually comfortable even though their eternal lives are in jeopardy.

A few years ago I was told in a vision that the church in America was almost completely unprepared for difficulties, and that great difficulties were coming. I knew the times of trouble would not be difficult for those who were prepared for them. In the years since receiving this word, I have come to understand that this preparation is basically walking in the biblical fear of the Lord. We can see this in the many promises that are given to those who fear Him.

Surely the Lord GOD does nothing unless He reveals His secret counsel to His servants the prophets (Amos 3:7).

Wouldn't you like to be one of those to whom the Lord revealed His secret counsel before He would do anything? Psalm 25:14 says, **"The secret of the Lord is for those who *fear* Him."** The one characteristic that is profoundly evident in the lives of all of the prophets was the pure and holy fear of the Lord. It could be accurately said that the fear of the Lord is the foundation of the prophetic ministry, and must be evident in all who desire to know the secret of the Lord.

Behold, the eye of the LORD is upon them that fear him, upon them that hope in his mercy (Psalm 33:18 KJV).

Of course, the Lord knows everything that goes on in the earth, but this phrase, to have your eye upon someone, revealed a special affection and care. David gave this exhortation in Psalm 34:

The angel of the LORD encamps around those who fear Him, and rescues them.
O taste and see that the LORD is good; How blessed is the man who takes refuge in Him!
O fear the LORD, you His saints; for to those who fear Him, there is no want.
The young lions do lack and suffer hunger; but they who seek the LORD shall not be in want of any good thing (Psalm 34:7-10).

The following are Scriptures that promise that which is greater than any earthly treasure we could accumulate. I encourage you to read them patiently and let them stir in you a heart to seek the fear of the Lord, that you might seek Him and find Him.

Thou hast given a banner to those who fear Thee, that it may be displayed because of the truth. Selah.
That Thy beloved may be delivered (Psalm 60:4-5).

For Thou hast been a refuge for me, a tower of strength against the enemy.
Let me dwell in Thy tent forever; let me take refuge in the shelter of Thy wings.
For Thou hast heard my vows, O God; thou hast given me the inheritance of those who fear Thy name (Psalm 61:3-5).

Surely His salvation is near to those who fear Him, that glory may dwell in our land (Psalm 85:9).

For as high as the heavens are above the earth, so great is his lovingkindness [mercy] toward those who fear Him;
Just as a father has compassion on his children, so the LORD has compassion on those who fear Him (Psalm 103:11, 13).

He will fulfill the desire of those who fear Him; He will also hear their cry and will save them (Psalm 145:19).

The LORD favors those who fear Him, those who wait for His lovingkindness (Psalm 147:11).

The fear of the LORD prolongs life (Proverbs 10:27).

In the fear of the LORD there is strong confidence, and his children will have refuge.
The fear of the LORD is a fountain of life, that one may avoid the snares of death (Proverbs 14:26-27).

Better is a little with the fear of the LORD, than great treasure and turmoil with it (Proverbs 15:16).

The fear of the LORD leads to life, so that one may sleep satisfied, untouched by evil (Proverbs 19:23).

The reward of humility and the fear of the LORD are riches, honor and life (Proverbs 22:4).

"But for you who fear My name the sun of righteousness will rise with healing in its wings; and you will go forth and skip about like calves from the stall.
And you will tread down the wicked, for they shall be ashes under the soles of your feet on the day which I am preparing," says the LORD of hosts (Malachi 4:2-3).

Have you noticed that many of the promises that it is so popular today to "claim," are conditional upon us having the fear of the Lord? Could this be why many spend endless hours memorizing the promises and quoting them without result? Some even use these promises to dictate orders to the Lord! Does that reflect the proper fear of the Lord? Presumption often has the appearance of authority, but it is a profound folly.

The Honor of His Presence

We can have a pure heart for the Lord, and yet still walk in the folly of presumption, just as King David did when he tried to bring the ark of God to Jerusalem (see II Samuel 6:1-11). The ark represents the glory of God's manifest presence. David just assumed that he could bring up the ark on a new ox cart.

Assumption is a basic characteristic of presumption, and those who assume are lacking in a basic respect for authority. The ox represents carnal strength, and there are many who believe that they can bring in the glory of God with their own strength and wisdom, though they would never say it. That presumption is not just foolish—it is deadly!

Uzzah was a faithful and good man. He, too, obviously had a heart for the Lord. When the ox cart was nearly upset, Uzzah reached out his hand to steady the ark. That seems like a very noble thing to do, but the anger of the Lord burned against Uzzah so that He struck him dead! Uzzah means "strength," and he thought that he could in his own strength steady the glory of God—a terrible presumption which he paid for with his life. Even so, David had set the stage for such a catastrophe by the way that he had tried to bring the ark up.

David first became angry, and then he got wise: **"So David was afraid of the LORD that day; and he said, 'How can the ark of the LORD come to me?' " (II Samuel 6:9).** It was wise of David to fear the Lord. It was also wise of him not to give up because of this one mistake, even though it was so tragic.

The Lord is pouring out His Spirit today in a seemingly unprecedented manner. There are many "Davids" who have sought Him and have a great passion to see His glory returned to the church, and the Lord wants to come. However, many are succumbing to the same mistake that David made. The casualness, and even arrogance, with which some have begun to handle His presence are preparing the way for terrible consequences if there is not quick repentance.

After the outbreak of the Lord at Perez-uzzah, David stopped everything until he had sought the Lord to know the way that He wanted to be moved. He brought the priests who would carry the ark according to the prescribed manner. Then, instead of trying to use the ox to bring Him to Jerusalem, David sacrificed an ox and a fatling every six paces (see verse 13). We will never bring the glory of the Lord to the church by our own strength. If we are wise we will sacrifice to the Lord whatever strength we have, just as Paul exhorted:

> **I urge you therefore, brethren, by the mercies of God, to present your bodies a living and holy sacrifice, acceptable to God, which is your spiritual service of worship.**
>
> **And do not be conformed to this world, but be transformed by the renewing of your mind, that you may prove what the will of God is, that which is good and acceptable and perfect.**
>
> **For through the grace given to me I say to every man among you not to think more highly of himself than he ought to think; but to think so as to have sound judgment, as God has allotted to each a measure of faith (Romans 12:1-3).**

> **You are not to say, "It is a conspiracy!" in regard to all that this people call a conspiracy, and you are not to fear what they fear or be in dread of it.**
>
> **It is the LORD of hosts whom you should regard as holy. *And He shall be your fear, and He shall be your dread. Then He shall become a sanctuary* (Isaiah 8:12-14).**

When we have the true and holy fear of the Lord, we do not have to fear anything else on this earth. To have the true fear of the Lord is evidenced by our not fearing what the world fears. God has never lost an election because He doesn't even compete in them! His policy in our country will not be dictated from Washington. But those who have authority with God through prayer, can dictate policy in Washington, regardless of who is in the office. **"For the LORD is our judge, the LORD is our lawgiver, the LORD is our King" (Isaiah 33:22 KJV).** Here we see that the Lord is all three branches of government.

When the church becomes like Daniel, He will then deal with the government like He did Nebuchadnezzar. This man was even more ruthless than the most despised modern despots. He destroyed Jerusalem, the temple, built a great golden idol to himself, and would on a whim destroy multitudes. However, he bowed his knee when He saw the power of the God of Daniel. When we, like Daniel, refuse to defile ourselves with the food and drink of the heathen and to worship their idols, but will worship the Lord openly, regardless of the consequences, He will give us wisdom and power that will confound the heathen, and cause them to bow their knees to our God.

> **See to it that you do not refuse Him who is speaking. For if those did not escape when they refused him who warned them on earth, much less shall we escape who turn away from Him who warns from heaven.**
> **And His voice shook the earth then, but now He has promised, saying, "Yet once more I will shake not only the earth, but also the heaven."**
> **And this expression, "Yet once more," denotes the removing of those things which can be shaken, as of created things, in order that those things which cannot be shaken may remain.**
> **Therefore, since we receive a kingdom which cannot be shaken, let us show gratitude, by which we may offer to God an acceptable service with reverence and awe;**
> **FOR OUR GOD IS A CONSUMING FIRE (Hebrews 12:25-29).**

We have a kingdom that cannot be shaken, regardless of elections, wars, revolutions, or even natural disasters. If we shake when the world shakes it is because we are building on the wrong foundation.

Therefore thus says the Lord GOD, "Behold, I am laying in Zion a stone, a tested stone, a costly cornerstone for the foundation, firmly placed. *He who believes in it* [Him] *will not be disturbed"* (Isaiah 28:16).

For a child will be born to us, a son will be given to us; and the government will rest on His shoulders. And His name will be called Wonderful Counselor, Mighty God, Eternal Father, Prince of Peace.

There will be no end to the increase of His government or of peace, on the throne of David and over His kingdom, to establish it and to uphold it with justice and righteousness from then on and forevermore. The zeal of the LORD of hosts will accomplish this (Isaiah 9:6-7).

PART II

Spiritual Authority

For readers of *The Morning Star Journal* and some of my other recent books, the following chapters on spiritual authority and witchcraft will be familiar. I felt to include them once again in this book, for the sake of those who have not read the other works, and because their message is essential for those who are called to walk in spiritual power to understand. These chapters have also been rewritten to be viewed from the perspective of ministry, and there have been some new insights added. I think you will find the review beneficial.

CHAPTER TEN

Kingdom Authority

We have come to the time of the greatest conflict between light and darkness that the earth has ever witnessed. It is the conflict of the ages. This is not a time to fear. We stand under the banner which has already won. The cross is the power of God, and His power is about to be revealed as never before on this earth. It is the time to take our stand with the absolute commitment to never retreat before the enemies of the cross. The cross of Jesus Christ will prevail against all of its enemies, and we are coming to the time when it will be made manifest.

The Lord said that **"the harvest is the end of the age" (Matthew 13:39).** This harvest is the reaping of everything that has been sown, both the good and the evil. The most glorious, and powerful, church will soon confront the deepest darkness. Cult and New Age powers are increasing dramatically, but the Lord has not left His people without power to face this evil onslaught. **"When the enemy shall come in like a flood, the spirit of the LORD shall lift up a standard against him" (Isaiah 59:19 KJV).** As cultish supernatural power has been growing, the supernatural power given to the church is increasing even more.

Cults have begun receiving supernatural revelation about Christian leaders in order to begin systematic attacks on them. The Lord has begun raising up prophets to discern the enemy's schemes so that the church can start to ambush him *before* he tries to implement his evil strategy. This is happening with more frequency and gives those who are open to this ministry a significant advantage in the battle.

We do not have to keep getting blind-sided by the enemy. The Lord is raising up an army that is going on the offensive, that will attack the strongholds of the enemy with weapons that are divinely powerful. We must not cower before the New Age and other cults, but see them as harvest fields!

However, as we proceed toward the conclusion of this age, the conflict between the light and darkness will become more supernatural. The day of supernatural neutrality is over. If we do not know the true power of God's Spirit we will become increasingly subject to the power of the evil one. Those whose fears or doctrines have led them to avoid even the supernatural power of God will find themselves, and their children, easy prey to evil supernatural power.

We must recognize the nature of the battle that we are in, and fight so as to win. We have come to the time when Satan and his hosts are being cast out of heaven and are coming down to the earth with great wrath. They will not fight fair and they will not fight on human terms—they will fight with every bit of power they have. The church must be equipped with every bit of power that the Lord intended for us to have in order to effectively fight this battle.

Men Were Created to Walk In the Supernatural

Men were created to have fellowship with God who is Spirit. Those who worship Him can *only* worship Him in Spirit and Truth. Because the purpose of man's creation is to have fellowship with God who is Spirit, and to worship (serve) Him in Spirit, there exists within him a void which draws him to the spiritual and supernatural. If this is not fulfilled by the Spirit of Truth, we will be deceived by the spirit of error. The spiritual vacuum in man will be filled. As C. S. Lewis declared, "If you deny a man food, he will gobble poison." If we deny men the right supernatural relationship with God they will succumb to the oppression or seductions of evil supernatural power.

The Test

God does not tempt men, but He does test them. These tests are for the purpose of promotion. Just as you had to pass tests to prove that you were qualified to advance to the next level in school, there are tests allowed by God in our lives so that He can trust us with more spiritual authority.

Tests are not for the Lord; He already knows what is in our heart. They are for us. The tests are not just for the purpose of revealing to us what is in our hearts, but for changing our hearts. The tests mold us into vessels that are fit for the Master's use. A primary test which everyone called to walk in true spiritual authority must pass is the rejection test.

The rejection test must have been the most difficult task for the Lord Himself to endure. Not only did He endure the desertion of almost all of His disciples when He needed them the most, but He also had to endure being forsaken by the Father as He took on the sin of the world. The One who was called to the highest position of authority had to pass the most difficult rejection test. This is because authority is basically about how we will relate to other people, and the Lord, when we have been given power and influence. This test will separate those who remain true because their heart is true, from those who only remain obedient for as long as it is politically expedient. The more spiritual authority that we are called to walk in, the greater this test will usually be in our life.

All authority, power and dominion have been given to Jesus because He was completely obedient. We will be trusted with authority, power and dominion to the degree that we are obedient. The true ministry of Jesus is a power ministry. He **"began to do and teach" (Acts 1:1).** We are called to be like Him and to do the works that He did. We must have power to do this. To be entrusted with this power we must be proven faithful. We must love the truth more than we love human approval or recognition. We must love it even more than we love our own lives.

There can be a corrupting force in power. It is often said that "Power corrupts, and absolute power corrupts absolutely." There is truth to this, which is why we must be tested so thoroughly before we will be trusted with real power.

There is at this time also a great release of counterfeit power in the New Age and other cults. They emphasize supernatural experiences which are demonic in origin, that are the counterparts similar biblical experiences. They mimic the power that men and women of God are called to walk in. Of course, the only reason why there is counterfeit money is because there is real money. Satan is using this for his own reasons, but the Lord is allowing it to test those who must walk in more power to accomplish His last day ministry.

Such an increase of the demonic activity exists because there is an increase of the real. This is intended to confuse the church so that she will reject the real gifts and experiences. Satan knows very well the impact that these gifts will have in helping the church to accomplish God's purpose in this last hour. Satan is attempting through this demonic activity to seduce Christians who are called to walk in supernatural power, but who are often rejected or misunderstood by the church and do not know or understand the power ministry of the Holy Spirit. Those who do not do well with the rejection test will always be vulnerable to seduction from the enemy.

Rejection comes to every man and woman of God. He allows it to come upon His ministers so that they can more fully identify with Him. The most noble and pure Man who ever walked the earth was constantly rejected, scorned, lied about, and ultimately even betrayed, denied and abandoned by His own best friends. As He explained, disciples are not above their master; if it happened to Him it will also happen to us. But this is our opportunity! It is through the greatest injustices that the greatest love can be demonstrated.

How many of us, if we knew that the next day all of our best friends were going to deny that they even knew us, would care to spend a last evening with them? He even washed their feet. Jesus loved His own regardless of their behavior. He was faithful even when they were not. There is no greater opportunity for us to grow in the true love of God than when we are rejected or abused. Jesus asked the Father to forgive even those who crucified Him. Stephen asked the same forgiveness for those who were stoning him.

God is love and those who minister in His Spirit will minister in love. The greater the love, the greater the power with which we can be entrusted. God allows rejection in our lives to help separate us from our own evil motives and to give us opportunities to grow in His love. If we feel rejected when people reject us it only reveals that we are not yet dead to this world—it is impossible for a dead man to feel rejection! Rejection accompanies with true ministry and rejection is one of our greatest opportunities to operate in true ministry, which is to demonstrate the true love of God. To be able to handle rejection without being offended is one of the great demonstrations of spiritual maturity, which is simply Christlikeness.

Many who were called as true prophets of God have been seduced by the enemy because they refused the protection and covering of the rest of the body of Christ. These have often refused the covering of the church because the leadership of the church misunderstood and sometimes rejected them. Again, the Lord allows this misunderstanding because learning to deal properly with rejection and authority is essential for anyone who is going to carry the awesome power and responsibility of having supernatural knowledge or revelation.

Most of what is called "discernment" in the church today is really suspicion, often motivated by jealousy or territorial preservation. This is why so many good and true ministries are attacked by other Christians. Anything but love will distort our discernment, which is why Paul explained to the Philippians that *"your love may abound* still **more and more** *in real knowledge and all discernment"* (Philippians 1:9).

God is love, and if we are going to speak for Him we must also abide in His love. His love is sometimes severe; sometimes it is His love that brings discipline, but it is still love. Even God's judgment is a manifestation of His love. We only have true spiritual authority in areas where He has given us His love.

Only when we are ministering from a foundation of His love will our ministry be true.

Romans 11:29 states: **"For the gifts and calling of God are without repentance"** (KJV). The Lord is faithful even when we are unfaithful. When the Lord gives a gift he will not take it back, even if we become unfaithful or misuse it. This is why men who may have gifts of healing or miracles can fall into sin or corruption but the gifts will still work. The same is true of the prophetic gifts of the Spirit. Because of this it is crucial that we not judge a ministry by the gift, but by the fruit. Those who move in the power and revelatory gifts who are affected by rejection or rebellion can use the gifts of God to bring division and damage to the very work of God. This is a dynamic which may be hard to understand, but is required because of the faithfulness of the Lord.

Under the Old Covenant a priest was not allowed to minister if he had scabs (see Leviticus 21:20). A scab is an unhealed wound. No one could touch a person with scabs. The same is true of us; when we have unhealed spiritual wounds others cannot get close to us and we cannot function in our true priestly ministry. Most of us have witnessed those who preach, prophesy or minister out of their own rejection, bitterness or other unhealed wounds—it is a corruption of their ministry. Until we can handle rejection and other injustices without being wounded, we are not ready for the spiritual priesthood that is the foundation of all true ministry.

The Foundation of Spiritual Authority

Paul explained to Timothy, **"The goal of our instruction is love from a pure heart and a good conscience and a sincere faith" (I Timothy 1:5).** Paul exhorted the Corinthians to **"earnestly desire spiritual gifts" (I Corinthians 14:1),** but he never exhorted them to make gifts their ultimate goal. We need the gifts and the power of the Spirit, and the church needs them much more than she presently knows. Even so, we need them for the sake of ministering to hurting people, not just to establish our ministries or to have big conferences.

When we lose sight of the goal, which is love, a pure heart, a good conscience, and a sincere faith, we have lost our way.

All of the gifts of the Spirit operate by faith, including prophecy, and faith works through love (see Galatians 5:6). True faith is not just the confidence that God *can* do certain things, it is knowing *why* He wants to do them. Fear is the counter to faith, but **"there is no fear in love; but perfect love casts out fear" (I John 4:18).** Love casts out everything that hinders the move of God through us, and to us. Love is the foundation upon which spiritual authority, and, thereby, the gifts of the Spirit, operates. It is vain to seek the gifts until they have a foundation upon which to be built. The strength of the foundation determines the level of power with which we can be trusted.

The Gifts Are God's Love

It has become a popular saying that we should not seek the gifts, but the Giver. This sounds noble, but it is contrary to the Word of God which exhorts us to **"pursue love, yet desire earnestly spiritual gifts" (I Corinthians 14:1).** The gifts of the Spirit and love are not mutually exclusive. We should pursue love and the fruit of the Spirit first, but that does not mean that we should not pursue the gifts as well—we should pursue both.

He expresses His love to us through the gifts of the Holy Spirit. We should *"desire earnestly"* the gifts, and do it because we love. Jesus healed the sick because He loved them and did not want them to suffer needlessly. He gave words of knowledge because He loved the people and wanted to impact them with the reality that God really did know them. The gifts of the Spirit enabled Jesus to do something, not just feel something, with His love.

The Lord gave the gifts to the church so that we could be extensions of His love and desire to minister to needy people. Jesus worked some of His great miracles in obscurity, and then He would even tell those healed not to tell anyone, but to go to the temple and offer thanksgiving to God. Jesus did not use the gifts of the Spirit just for impressing people, but for loving them and touching them in their place of need.

If Jesus had just wanted to impress people with the power of God, He could have given the Jews a sign from heaven just as they asked. In asking for a sign from heaven, the Jews were not just asking for another miracle, but they were asking Him to do something in the sky, to stop the sun like Joshua did, or make the shadow reverse as Isaiah did. The Lord could have easily done that, and He could do it today if He wanted just to impress people with His power. Impressing people with His power is not the primary reason for the gifts of the Spirit—love for people is the reason for them.

Satan tempted Jesus by trying to get Him to use the power of God for selfish reasons, or to testify of who He was. The truth is that the power He was given *was* meant to testify of who He was, but it was crucial that He not try to do that Himself, but that He let the Father do it. Jesus was focused entirely on glorifying the Father, and the Father was focused entirely on glorifying His Son—neither was trying to glorify Himself.

The Lord does use His supernatural power to verify His word and those He has sent, but we must trust Him to do that. Whenever we seek the gifts in order to testify of our own ministries, we are in the process of falling from grace. We must utterly devote ourselves to testifying of Jesus and making His name great, and leave the confirming of our ministries entirely to Him.

Many seek after a miracle because they know how that miracle will impact unbelieving relatives or friends. It is true that some miracles will impact unbelievers, but most will not be impressed, regardless of how spectacular they are. Even after Jesus raised Lazarus from the dead the Jews just sought even more to kill Him. When unbelievers are impacted by miracles it is a wonderful bonus, but we will miss the point if we are seeking miracles or power ministry just to impress people. I have rarely seen the Lord do a great miracle when that was the primary motive.

True Maturity Is Love

We are tested through rejection and misunderstanding so that we can overcome rejection. If we are to accomplish the purposes of God, we must come to the level of maturity where **"the love of Christ controls us" (II Corinthians 5:14).** Love has not taken into account the wrongs suffered and is not motivated by rejection, which drives us either to retaliation or to try to prove ourselves.

Spiritual gifts which are not motivated by love are **"a noisy gong or a clanging cymbal" (I Corinthians 13:1).** Gifts of the Spirit which are not grounded in love are usually *noisy*. These will come with fanfare and hype, founded upon self-promotion. A noisy gong or clanging cymbal will also make the real trumpet more difficult to hear. But one who is controlled by the love of Christ will be consumed by the one desire to see Him glorified and worshipped.

True love is tolerant and patient. There is certainly a place for calling the church to maturity and to the obedience of Christ. This is a basic function of the prophetic ministry, but it must be done in love and not in impatience or intolerance. We occasionally need to look at where we ourselves were just five, ten or fifteen years ago. Are we being impatient with those who are at the same levels that we were then? Are we giving less grace to people than the Lord gave to us?

Much of the church is immature because it is supposed to be immature! A two year old child is immature and is supposed to be. It is perfectly acceptable for a two year old to wear diapers. Now if a fifteen year old is still having to wear them we have a problem. My two year old shouldn't try to do the things that my seven year old can do; expecting such maturity from him would only frustrate him, and could actually hinder his development. I want him to be disciplined, and mature for his age level, but I must not require more than that from him. We must have the same patience with the church. We must discern where people are and call them to the proper discipline and maturity commensurate with it.

Every ministry that is working for the equipping of the church must be careful not to put their personal expectations on the church, but to seek the Lord for His expectations. Ministers who have been through previous rejections, without being healed of them, often take their next assignment with a determination to prove themselves. This will cause them to put unrealistic pressures on themselves and those within their flock, which only leads to more failures. This can be a vicious cycle that leaves a long line of hurt people and a ministry that is either too bitter or too insecure to function.

Again, when we know that we have received our commission from above, and that we are known by the Father, it really does not matter what other men think of us. This is a liberation that is essential for any minister. We cannot function in true ministry if we are carrying any other yoke but the Lord's. We must not allow ourselves to be controlled by human expectations, even our own expectations, but only by the Lord's. He does not expect of us what He does not empower us to perform.

Jesus experienced the greatest rejection the world has ever known or will know. He was rejected by the world that He Himself had made. He came in love, healing and delivering the oppressed, and He never once committed a sin. Yet, He suffered the most cruel and humiliating death, and He suffered it for the very ones who killed Him. He turned the greatest evil and the greatest injustice the world had ever known into the opportunity to forgive and save the very ones who persecuted Him.

The Lord commanded those who followed Him to do the same thing—we must take up our crosses every day just as He did. If we do that we have the power to overcome evil with good. Every evil that is done has the counterbalancing power to be used for good that will deliver men from the evil that is in them. As ministers of the gospel we are meant to be rejected, but we must turn each rejection into an opportunity to show the love of God.

Authority for Healing

It is by the Lord's stripes that we are healed. The same principle is true for us as well. In the very place where we are wounded we can receive authority for healing. If we have been abused we will receive authority for healing others who are abused once we are healed. Even when we are healed we will remain sensitive in that area. This sensitivity becomes discernment so that we will quickly recognize others who have suffered as we have. This sensitivity also enables us to minister in the compassion that is required for true ministry.

It is for this reason that the Lord allowed every wound that we have suffered in our lives—so that He could give us authority for healing in those same areas. That is why Paul pointed to his wounds and tribulations when his authority was questioned. Don't waste your trials! They really are more precious than gold. What value could ever be placed upon a single healing?

There is a point at which men reject the love and mercy of the Lord to the degree that they become incorrigible—meaning they are beyond help. This happened to Judas. At this point, God's mercy is replaced with judgment. But we must understand that **"mercy triumphs over judgment" (James 2:13).**

The Lord's patience with men usually greatly exceeds what we are willing to endure before pronouncing judgment. Just as almost any parent is going to be far more patient with his own children than he will with others, the Lord is usually far more patient with men because they are His children. He sent His own Son to be tortured and killed for them because He loves them. If the Son of God could suffer the cruelty and injustice that He did for our sakes, how much more should we be willing to suffer for the sake of extending His great salvation?

CHAPTER ELEVEN

Counterfeit Spiritual Authority

Overcoming witchcraft is one of the primary battles that almost everyone called to the ministry must face. Many are not even aware of this power that is almost certainly arrayed against them, and therefore they suffer many needless wounds from it. One of the important biblical personifications of this battle is found in the struggle between Elijah and Jezebel—the quintessential prophet versus the ultimate witch.

This battle is so crucial to those called to the ministry that it's outcome will determine whether or not they will fulfill their calling. Even Elijah suffered such a setback in his battle with Jezebel that he had to pass his mantle on to another, and Elisha had to later fulfill many of the commissions that God had given to Elijah.

Elijah still accomplished a great deal. He was still one of the greatest prophets who ever lived, and received the extraordinary honor of being carried to heaven in a chariot of fire. However, he still did not accomplish all that had been given him to do. Regardless of how much we have done, the spirit of Jezebel will come against us to keep us from completing our mission.

We do not want to unnecessarily lift up the enemy, and it is not biblical for us to fear the enemy, but we must know and understand his schemes or we will likely be foiled by them. The spirit of Jezebel is one of his most powerful weapons against anyone who walks in spiritual authority, and if we do not respect that power, it will hit us very hard at a most inappropriate time.

Right after Elijah's greatest victory, after fearlessly confronting and then slaying hundreds of false prophets, this one woman, Jezebel, declares that she is going to get him and Elijah flees for his life. He then comes under such depression that he does not even want to live. Those who underestimate the power of the Jezebel spirit are in for a terrible shock, and probably a terrible defeat. I have personally witnessed many churches destroyed, and many great men of God undone by this terrible guile.

Witchcraft has dramatically increased throughout the world in recent years. One of the expressed goals of this movement is to dilute, subjugate and destroy biblical Christianity. Many Christians are presently suffering attacks in some form from those who practice witchcraft. Discerning the nature of these attacks and knowing how to overcome them is becoming important for all believers, not just prophets. But prophets will unquestionably be on the forefront of this battle just as Elijah was in his time.

Our Advantage In the Battle

We are not to be ignorant of the enemy's schemes (see II Corinthians 2:11), but **"let us be on the alert. Your adversary, the devil, prowls about like a roaring lion, seeking someone to devour. But resist him, firm in your faith" (I Peter 5:8-9).** Understanding Satan's schemes significantly increases our advantage in the battle. Being on the Lord's side assures the final victory. The church will win, the gospel will ultimately prevail. The issue for us is whether this will happen through us, or will it be our successors who witness the ultimate victory?

The entire church age has been one of spiritual warfare and it is intensifying as the end approaches. Satan is now being cast out of the heavenlies and down to the earth where he is coming with great wrath. Even so, we need not fear—He who is in us is *much greater* than he who is in the world. He who is least in the kingdom of God has more power than any antichrist.

But just as the greatest military power today is vulnerable if it does not recognize the enemy's attack, we, too, are vulnerable if we do not recognize Satan's schemes. The only way that he can defeat us is through our own ignorance or complacency. As we maintain our position in Christ, taking on the full armor of God and remaining vigilant, we will not only stand but will prevail against the gates of hell.

What Is Witchcraft?

Witchcraft is basically counterfeit spiritual authority; it is using an evil spirit to dominate, manipulate or control others. The apostle Paul named witchcraft (also called "sorcery") as one of the works of the flesh (see Galatians 5:20). It does have its origin in the carnal nature though it usually degenerates quickly into demonic power. When we try to use emotional pressure to manipulate others it is a basic form of witchcraft. When we use hype or soul power to enlist service, even for the work of God, it is witchcraft. When businessmen scheme to find pressure points while pursuing a deal, this, too, can be witchcraft. Many of the manipulative tactics promoted as sales tactics in market-ing are basic forms of witchcraft. This is one reason why the New Age Movement is making such inroads into the ranks of professionals—they recognize real power.

The basic defense against counterfeit spiritual authority is to walk in true spiritual authority. Overcoming witchcraft is sim-ple, but it is not easy. It is as simple as entering into the rest of God and taking His yoke upon us. That is why the apostle Paul warned the church, **"But I fear, lest by any means, as the serpent beguiled [literally, "bewitched"] Eve through his subtlety, so your minds should be corrupted *from the simplicity that is in Christ"* (II Corinthians 11:3 KJV).**

We are bewitched primarily by being led away from the simplicity of devotion to Christ. What we call "charismatic witchcraft" (this is not meant to denote any movement or group of people) usually gains entry to a church or ministry through selfish ambition. This will lead us to start striving to build, thereby causing us to depart from the rest of God, taking upon ourselves yokes that are not His.

Everything that God gives us to do He empowers us to do. Everything that we begin in our own strength must be maintained by our own strength, which leads to pressure, manipulation and control. Establishing our lives on truth and trusting the Lord to accomplish what concerns us is essential if we are ever to be free of the influence and pressure of witchcraft.

The True Seat of Authority

It is written that Jesus is seated upon the throne of David. This is, of course, a metaphor as Jesus does not sit upon the literal throne that David sat on. David established a position of true spiritual authority that would ultimately issue in the kingdom of God. David did for spiritual authority what Abraham did for faith. How did David establish a seat of true authority? He simply refused to take authority or seek influence for himself, but utterly trusted in God to establish him in the position that was ordained for him. David did not lift his own hand to seek recognition or influence, and neither must we if we are going to walk in true spiritual authority and not mere human political power.

Any authority or influence that we gain by our own manipulation or self-promotion will be a stumbling block to us, hindering our ability to receive a true commission and authority from God. If we are going to walk in true spiritual authority, like David, we will have to utterly trust in the Lord to establish us in it and in His time. As Peter exhorted, **"Humble yourselves, therefore, under the mighty hand of God,** *that He may exalt you at the proper time"* **(I Peter 5:6).**

There is possibly nothing more devastating to our calling and potential for walking in true ministry than seeking influence or authority prematurely. Premature success can be one of the most dangerous things that can happen to us. Even though David had been called and anointed as the king many years before, he was completely patient in waiting for the position. David did not call himself the king, he let God do it, and he waited *patiently* for the people to recognize God's will. In contrast, Jezebel *"calls herself* **a prophetess"** **(Revelation**

2:20). We must beware of anyone who is seeking to establish his own recognition in ministry.

When the Lord promotes, He also supplies the grace and wisdom to carry the authority. There is no greater security available than knowing that God knows us and He has established our ministry. There is little that can breed insecurity faster than trying to maintain a position that we gained by our own promotion or manipulation, which is the root of probably most of the territorial preservation and divisions that presently exist in the body of Christ.

Being established in true spiritual authority is a fortress that just cannot be penetrated by the enemy. Paul explained that **"the *God of peace* will soon crush Satan under your feet" (Romans 16:20).** When we know that we have been established by God we have a peace that utterly crushes the enemy. Those who have established themselves in a position of authority, or influence, have little peace. The more our illegally gained influence increases, the more striving and manipulating it will take to hold it together. Anything that we do through manipulation, hype, or soul power, regardless of how noble or spiritual our goals are, is done in the counterfeit spiritual authority of witchcraft and is doomed to ultimate failure.

Therefore, the first principle in being delivered from the influence of witchcraft, is to repent of all of the ways that we ourselves have used it. Satan cannot cast out Satan. Witchcraft, in even its most evil and diabolical forms, will have an open door into our lives if we ourselves are using it by manipulating or controlling for the sake of gaining a position.

We may be using such devices under the seemingly justified reasoning of trying to build the church, but God is not fooled and neither is the enemy. What God is building is not raised up by human might or power, but by His Spirit. Whatever we build by any other means is an affront to the cross and will ultimately oppose that which the Spirit is doing. The flesh wars against the Spirit, regardless of how good we try to make the flesh look.

The Gift of Discernment

The gift of discernment of spirits is a primary gift of the Holy Spirit enabling us to distinguish the spiritual source of influences in the church. Much of what is called "discernment" today is really *suspicion* rooted more in a territorial spirit of self-preservation than in the Holy Spirit. This is because so much of the authority that is exercised in the church today is counterfeit, which causes those who use it to be striving, fearful and intimated by anyone that they cannot control.

True spiritual discernment is rooted in love that is "patient, kind, not jealous, does not brag, is not arrogant, does not act unbecomingly, does not seek its own, is not provoked, does not take into account a wrong suffered, does not rejoice in unrighteousness, but rejoices in the truth; bears all things, believes all things, hopes all things, endures all things" (see I Corinthians 13:4-7). Many consider that the readiness to "believe all things, hope all things and endure all things" will lead to more of a naiveté than to discernment, but the reverse is actually true. Unless we are seeing through the eyes of God's love we are not seeing clearly and we will not interpret accurately what we see.

True discernment can only operate through God's love. God's love is not to be confused with unsanctified mercy which gives approval to the things that God disapproves of. God's love is utterly pure and easily distinguishes between the pure and the impure, and it always does it for the right reasons. Insecurity, self-preservation, self-promotion, unhealed wounds, unforgiveness, bitterness, etc. will all confuse and neutralize true spiritual discernment.

Spiritual Maturity

Learning to overcome rejection and misunderstanding just as the Lord did, by praying for the forgiveness of His persecutors, is essential if we are to walk in the Spirit, in true spiritual authority, or a true ministry.

If we are to accomplish the purposes of God, we must come to the level of maturity where **"the love of Christ controls** us" (II Corinthians 5:14). Love does not take into account wrongs suffered and is not motivated by rejection, which drives us to retaliation in the attempt to prove ourselves, and leads to a fall from walking in true authority.

Self-Promotion Leads to Divination

The over-promotion of one's gift is a sure sign that there may also be other destructive problems in that person's ministry, even if the gift is real. A prophet who promotes himself will usually end up crossing the line between revelation and divination. True revelation comes to those who are yielded and submissive to the Lord, not through striving for it.

Prophetic experiences do not testify to one's maturity or importance. Mature prophets will be given more to seeking a relationship and intimacy with the Lord than to experiences. Those who strive to have experiences may well succeed in having them, but from the wrong source. Revelation will come to a true prophet without striving. An apple tree does not worry about how many apples it will produce each day; if it is a real apple tree, apples will come.

However, we must also distinguish between *seeking* and *striving*. It is right to seek the gifts of the Spirit, but that does not mean that we must strive for them. True seekers will be at peace and rest, not agitated. I prayed for 25 years to be caught up into the third heaven as Paul was before I began having experiences approaching that level. It is through faith and patience that we receive the promises (see Hebrews 6:12). True faith is demonstrated by patience. Faith seeks, but it also rests and trusts in the wisdom of God.

Every bit of influence that we gain through self-promotion will someday become a snare to us. All of the money or other resources that we raise through self-promotion will actually become a stumbling block to our walking in the ministry to which we have been called.

Whatever is gained by striving and self-promotion will have to be sustained by the same, which will keep us from walking in the place where God has called us, not to mention misleading whoever is naive enough to follow us. Manipulation and hype are deadly enemies, not only to the prophetic ministry, but to all true ministry. Anyone who understands true ministry and true spiritual authority will not want one bit of influence that God does not give to them.

The Fear of Man Leads to Witchcraft

King Saul is a good example of how a person with a true ministry and anointing from God can fall into this counterfeit spiritual authority, or witchcraft. When he was commanded to wait for Samuel before offering the sacrifice, he succumbed to the pressure and offered it prematurely. He said, **"I saw that the people were scattering from me . . . and that the Philistines were assembling" (I Samuel 13:11).** It is at this same point many who fall depart from the course; when we begin to fear the people or the circumstances more than we fear God, we will fall from walking in true authority. When we start to fear the people leaving more than we fear God leaving, we have departed from true faith.

Crossing the Line

It is noteworthy that Saul transgressed by offering sacrifices to God that he was not qualified to offer. Saul was from the tribe of Benjamin, not Levi. This is how witchcraft usually causes us to stumble, by compelling us to go beyond our designated realm of authority. Paul the apostle explained that he did not presume to go beyond the sphere of authority that had been appointed to him to reach as far as Corinth. This was a geographical limit that God had placed upon him at that time, which was obviously later lifted, but Paul was careful not to cross it. When we get beyond what God has called us to do we get beyond His grace, and then we are easy targets for the enemy. If Satan cannot stop you, he will try to push you too far.

This was the downfall of some of the "mega-ministries" during the 1980s, but it has also been the downfall of countless smaller ones who were trying to keep up with them. This was the inevitable consequence of some of the distorted concepts of faith that were promoted during that time. True faith is not always demonstrated by getting bigger and better, but sometimes by ending what was even a promise of God, which Abraham was willing to do when he offered Isaac.

If you are called to be a captain of 500, you can increase your church attendance through promotions and good salesmanship, but even if you grow to 5,000, the day will come when church splits bring you right back to what you have the anointing for. The day will come when no amount of hype and soul power can hold the work together beyond what you have the grace for. The only way you can hold it beyond what you have the grace for is to become, to at least some degree, a cult.

Those who really understand spiritual authority will also have a profound understanding of God's grace. Their greatest fear will be to depart from that place of His grace. James and Peter understood this, which is why they both emphasized that **"God resists the proud, but gives grace to the humble" (James 4:6; see also I Peter 5:5).** It is pride that compels us to go beyond what God has called us to do. The ultimate form of this pride is the "I must save the world mentality." We may feel a real compassion when we try to respond to every human need, but it is a human compassion at best, and it has deceived us into trying to walk in something that even the Lord Jesus Himself said He did not do.

The Deadly Trap

Because witchcraft is basically rooted in the fear of man, and **"the fear of man is a snare" (Proverbs 29:25 KJV),** those who begin to operate in witchcraft are trapped—fear is the snare. The bigger the project or ministry that we have built with the hype, manipulation or control, the more we will fear anything or anyone that we cannot manipulate or control. Those who are caught in this deadly trap will fear those who walk in the true anointing and authority the most, because they are the least affected by the manipulation or control spirits.

This is why Saul became enraged at David and was consumed with destroying him, even though David was "but a flea" at the time. As the manipulation and control take dominion in our hearts, so will the paranoia. Those who have fallen into this deadly trap will become irrationally consumed at driving out or destroying anyone who threatens their control.

Those who receive their authority, recognition, or security from men will, like Saul, end up in the witch's house. That is why Samuel warned Saul that **"rebellion is as the sin of witchcraft" (I Samuel 15:23 KJV).** When one in spiritual authority rebels against the Holy Spirit, the void will be filled by the counterfeit spiritual authority of witchcraft.

This may begin as the simple reliance upon hype and soul power, but without repentance it can end up in the most diabolical forms of presumption and rebellion, as we see in the case of King Saul. Saul killed the true priests, persecuted the ones whose hearts were really after the Lord, and spent his last night in the house of a witch as the natural conclusion to the direction his life had taken.

Spiritual authority is a dangerous occupation. If we are wise, like David, we will not seek a position of authority, and we will not even take one which is offered until we are certain that the Lord is the One offering it. Satan tempts every one called by God with the same temptation he offered to Jesus; if we will bow down to him and his ways he will give us authority over kingdoms. God has called us to rule over kingdoms, too, but His way leads to the cross and can only be attained if we become servants of all. Satan's temptation is to offer the quick and easy path to what God has in fact called us to attain.

The Responsibility of True Authority

One of the most frequent phrases attributed to David was "*he inquired of the Lord.*" On the few occasions when David made a major decision without inquiring of the Lord, the consequences were devastating. It was not just David who suffered the consequences of this presumption, but the people who were under him. The higher the position of authority the more dangerous it is, and the more people who are affected by even the seemingly insignificant decisions.

When Adam fell billions of souls were to suffer. With authority comes very real responsibility. Only the most evil, perverted soul would crave such authority for selfish reasons. True spiritual authority is not an honor to be sought; it is a burden to be carried. Many who seek authority and influence do not know what they are asking for, and that their immaturity can be their doom if it is given to them before the time.

Even though David lived a thousand years before the age of grace, he knew grace possibly as well as anyone who has lived in this age. Yet, he, too, made mistakes which cost thousands of lives. It was probably because Solomon had observed his father, that the one thing he desired was wisdom to rule over God's people. Anyone called to a position of leadership in the church must be of the same devotion. Even without being in a position of spiritual authority, presumption can kill us. If we are in a position of authority it almost certainly will lead to our fall, and can lead to the fall of many others as well.

The gift of a word of knowledge can be an awesome demonstration of power, and does carry a great deal of excitement, but those who are called to walk in spiritual authority would do well to seek the gift of a word of wisdom even more than words of knowledge. We need the power of words of knowledge to accomplish the work of the Lord, but we must have the wisdom to use that power properly.

The Safety Net

Those who attain prominence before humility *will fall*, because **"God opposes the proud, but gives grace to the humble"** (James 4:6 NIV). Therefore, if we have wisdom we will seek humility before position. True authority operates on the grace of God, and the more authority we walk in the more grace we need.

We only have true spiritual authority to the degree that the King lives within us. True spiritual authority is not a position; it is a grace. Counterfeit spiritual authority stands on its position instead of grace. The highest spiritual authority, Jesus, used His position to lay down His life. He commanded those who would come after Him to take up their crosses to do the same.

There is a simple distinguishing factor between the false ministry and the true: the false use their gifts and the people for themselves; true ministries use their gifts and give themselves for the people. Again, self-seeking, self-promotion and self-preservation are the most destructive forces to true ministry. Even if we have been anointed by God like King Saul was, we, too, can fall to witchcraft if these gain control over us.

CHAPTER TWELVE

Our Shield Against Witchcraft

Not only must those in leadership be wary of using witch-craft, they must also be aware that they will be the primary target of those who do. It is an enemy we must watch for from within and without. It is just as subtle when it attacks from without as when it gains influence in our own hearts. This form of sorcery is seldom what we call black magic, but is usually a form of "white witchcraft." This includes well meaning people who do not have the confidence to be straight-forward and have there-fore fallen to subtle forms of manipulation to gain influence.

One prominent form of white witchcraft that is common in the church we call "charismatic witchcraft." This has possibly done more damage to the body of Christ than any other single factor, without yet being fully understood or combated. This is a pseudo-spirituality used to gain influence or control by using a super-spiritual mask. This is a source of false prophecies, dreams and visions which ultimately destroy or neutralize the work, or bring the leadership to the point where they overreact so as to despise prophecy altogether. The person using this form of witchcraft will almost always think that he has the mind of the Lord and that the leadership is in rebellion.

Flattery Will Get You Nowhere

Flattery is one of the most deadly tactics of the enemy, intended to divert a church or work from God's will. Prophets who have fallen into witchcraft through self-promotion will often be used by the enemy in this way. They will divert you from the course by prophesying that which is much more grand or appealing than what God has called you to. In this way the heart and the resources of the ministry will be sidetracked, and usually devastated by failure.

Beware of those who try to gain influence by prophesying grandiose visions. Receive such words only from those who have nothing to gain by sharing them, or whose integrity has been fully established, never from those who are trying to establish themselves. Prophets of extraordinary gifts and authority in this century have themselves been tripped up by others who prophesied to them that they were greater than they were, or were called to do things greater than they were called to do. On the day of judgment we may find that this form of witchcraft was far more devastating to the church than the attacks from cults, New Age, and all of the other false prophets combined.

It is very easy to discern false prophets who are from cults, but those who are in the church, who may be genuine believers, are much harder to distinguish. Yes, a true believer can still be a false prophet. We are false in any ministry that we presume without a commission from God. Prophetic authority cannot be established through any other credentials.

Letters of recommendation do have their place, but we should question anyone who tries to establish spiritual authority by what school they attended, the diplomas they have, or whose ministry they have sat under. Also, beware of those who are always telling stories of their own prophetic exploits. At best, this is evidence of immaturity. Those who are the real thing have kept company with God and His angels enough that they will not care very much about who else believes in them. If we are going to be free of the traps set by false prophets we must start recognizing self-promotion and rejecting the ministry of those who use it.

Resisting Witchcraft

The basic strategy we must use to begin freeing ourselves from the power of witchcraft is to *bless those who curse us*. This does not mean that we bless their works, but that we pray for them and not against them. In the case of the immature or unstable who have fallen to manipulation and self-promotion, we bless them by standing for truth and integrity without compromise. We can reject their ministry without rejecting them, but rather helping them to the path of deliverance and redemption.

We must also bless those who try to curse us with black magic or other forms of power. If the enemy can get us to retaliate he will then have us using the same spirit, and we will have multiplied the very evil we are trying to cast out. We are not warring against flesh and blood and the weapons of our warfare are not carnal, but spiritual. When we begin to pray blessing upon the people who are attacking us, then the evil power of control and manipulation is broken over them and us. We must not return evil for evil, but *overcome evil with good.*

Understanding New Age Witchcraft

The New Age Movement is basically a combination of witchcraft and Hinduism disguised to make it acceptable to white collar professionals. There is an important reason why this form of spiritualism is targeting this group. For almost 5,800 years of the earth's 6,000 year recorded history, nearly ninety-five percent of all workers were agricultural. In just a little over a century that statistic has been reversed, so that now less than five percent of the workers in the West are agricultural. This change was the result of technological advances. The five percent who work in agriculture now produce more than the ninety-five percent could in the last century.

In the mid-1950s, white collar workers exceeded the number of blue collar workers in the West. Since that time this majority has grown until it is now estimated that blue collar workers will go the way of agricultural workers in the near future, composing only a very small fraction of society. When the Lord predicted that "knowledge will increase" few understood the degree to which this would happen. Now information is the most valuable commodity in the world and the job of accumulating, interpreting, packaging and transferring knowledge is the largest industry on earth.

Those involved in the knowledge industry are not only the most numerous, but they are also the most wealthy and most powerful. They are also the group that the church has become unsuccessful in reaching. This has helped to feed the proliferation of the New Age and other cults. Because man was created to have fellowship with God who is Spirit, there is a spiritual void in man that creates a spiritual hunger for the supernatural. Those who do not know the true supernatural power of God will become drawn to the evil and counterfeit supernatural powers of the enemy.

Paul explained, **"For the kingdom of God does not consist in words, but in power" (I Corinthians 4:20).** Satan knows this and is quite content to fight the battle on the level of words (doctrines, etc.). Regardless of how true or how well we can argue about our doctrines, Satan has little problem conquering those who do not know the power of God, because these do not really know the kingdom of God—the kingdom does not consist of words, but power. Those who really believe the Bible will walk in power. Righteousness is the result of believing in our hearts, not our minds, and those who do not know the power of God only believe in Him in their minds.

In light of some of the foolishness that manifested itself in the Pentecostal, Charismatic, Full Gospel and Third Wave Movements, which have all known the power of God, it is easy to understand why many would shy away from the gifts of the Spirit. But this, too, is one of the tests that separate the true believers from those who just know creeds or doctrines. God has called the foolish things of the world to confound the wise. Only the humble will come to what He is doing and He will give His grace only to them.

Churches which have rejected the supernatural power of God today have become irrelevant and unable to reach a world in supernatural conflict. The more secularized society becomes the more it actually magnifies the hunger in man for fellowship with the supernatural.

This is why atheists tend to be drawn to the most base forms of witchcraft and the black arts; they are deceived into thinking that they are touching the powers that are resident within man, but are actually demonic. The denominations and movements within the church which have rejected the supernatural power of God are almost all shrinking as they have become irrelevant and boring to even their own people, with little or no power to attract converts.

Many of those churches and denominations that have rejected the power of God have already succumbed to influences from the New Age Movement. Others are succumbing to the spirit of the age in other forms, not only tolerating the perverted and unbelievers as members, but actually ordaining them as pastors and leaders. Contrary to this, the denominations and movements that preach and walk in the supernatural power of God are not only growing, but, when measured as a single group, are by far the fastest growing religious movement in the world.

Paul the apostle declared, **"My message and my preaching were not in persuasive words of wisdom, but in demonstration of the Spirit and power,** *that your faith should not rest on the wisdom of men, but on the power of God"* **(I Corinthians 2:4-5).** The conflict between the kingdom of God and the kingdom of evil is both a conflict between truth and error, and it is a supernatural power confrontation. Both sides of which are seeking to fill the spiritual void in man created by the fall.

The entire history of God's dealings with men have included demonstrations of supernatural power. It is a contradiction to claim to be a biblical people if we do not walk in the supernatural power of God. The Bible itself teaches that those who really believe it will do the things that are written in it. Probably the most dishonoring theology ever devised by powerless Christians essentially states that the Holy Spirit was an Author who wrote just one book and then retired! To imply that we do not need Him anymore because we have a book about Him is not only ludicrous, it is deception in the highest order. The Lord is the same today as He was when the Bible was written, and He is still doing everything that He did then.

True Christianity consists, not only of words, but of demonstrations of God's love and power to save, heal and deliver. Jesus stated that as the Father had sent Him into the world, He has sent us into the world (see John 17:18). Jesus did not just talk about God's power to heal and save, He demonstrated it. If we are going to preach the gospel we are to preach it as He did, demonstrating God's love and power. When He sent out His disciples it was to heal the sick and cast out demons as they preached the kingdom. He does not change and He has not changed the way He sends His true messengers.

Many of the biblical prophecies concerning the end of the age address the supernatural nature of the times. The church that does not walk in power will become increasingly inadequate for dealing with the times and confronting the powers that come against her. To overcome the power of the enemy, we must **"earnestly desire spiritual gifts, especially that you may prophesy" (I Corinthians 14:1).** The first defense against the deceptive supernatural power of the enemy is to know the true power of God.

Seeking Rightly

Most believers now desire spiritual gifts, but we must "earnestly" desire them if we are going to receive them. Even though most of the church is now "open" for God to use them in a demonstration of His power, He has decreed that one must *ask, seek* and *knock* in order to receive. Those who are just "open" for the Lord to use them almost never are actually used. Being "open" is usually a cop-out for those who are either too fearful or too prideful to risk failure. It takes faith and seeking, if we are to receive.

Jesus made the way for us to be as close to God as we want to be. There is not a single person in the Bible, history, or alive today who is closer to the Lord than you can be. The only difference between those who are close to God and those who are not is that those who are close want Him badly enough to seek Him. The same is true of everything that He offers to us in His word. Those who want the gifts of the Spirit badly enough will "earnestly desire" them enough to seek until they receive.

"But," we may ask, "Isn't that just self-promotion?" It can be. We can seek the gifts for the most base, selfish reasons, or we can seek them with the most pure motives. Most of us will fall somewhere between these extremes. I recognize very well that all of my motives are not pure, but I keep seeking out of obedience to His word, while praying for the Lord to correct my motives. We can perform any biblical discipline, such as praying, worshipping, even witnessing, out of selfish motives.

Does this mean that we should stop doing these things? Of course not! We seek to do them with different motives. But if we wait until our motives are perfect we will never do any of them. It is often by doing them that we are changed. We are not changed in order to come into the presence of the Lord, but we are changed by coming into His presence.

Seeking to walk in the gifts of the Spirit is one form of seeking God, and even more importantly, it is being obedient. Our God is supernatural and we cannot truly desire fellowship with Him without desiring fellowship with the supernatural. Even those who have been hardened by doctrines and try to justify their powerlessness, long in their hearts for the supernatural. They simply allow their fears to keep them from knowing God as He is—all powerful. We were all created for fellowship in the Spirit, which is supernatural or it would not be spiritual.

Truth and Power

Recently, some of the world's most brilliant theologians and apologists for why God no longer moves supernaturally, have begun to believe that He does, after witnessing just one genuine miracle. "Genuine" is the key word here. Many of those who love truth would seek to walk in the power of God if they had not been so turned off by the fakery and hype often associated with the ministry of those who really do not yet have power, but claim to.

True Christianity is the true word of God verified by the true power of God. Jesus went about to **"do and teach" (Acts 1:1).** He would perform miracles before He taught. He knew that people who had an undeniable encounter with God would be far more open to what He would say to them.

The power Jesus and His evangelists demonstrated was used to confirm and illuminate their teaching. The same is still true; the demonstrations of God's power transforms intellectual concepts into a true faith in His teachings. It takes both the word and the power of God to change the inner man. Without both, we may change our outward behavior but our hearts remain untouched. It is the spiritual void in the heart that must be filled by a true fellowship with God if we are going to be free of the spiritual influence and power of the enemy.

Because witchcraft is basically counterfeit spiritual authority, we will only be completely free from the power of witchcraft when we are completely submitted to the power and authority of God, which requires that we be utterly committed to truth. If the spiritual void that is in us is not filled with the real power and real authority of God, we will become dangerously subject to witchcraft in some form as we draw closer to the end of the age.

The Battle of Armageddon is fought in the "valley of decision"; that day everyone on earth will be brought to the place of making a decision. It is a power confrontation and the choice is being made over power and authority. We will choose the power and authority of God or the power and authority of the evil one—but we will all choose.

Discerning Counterfeits

Each of the gifts of the Spirit that are available to the church are presently counterfeited by the enemy. Those whose fears cause them to avoid spiritual gifts in order to keep from being deceived, are certain to be deceived. We must walk by faith, not fear, if we are going to stay on the path that leads to life. Fear will lead us to deception if we follow it; it takes a faith like Abraham's that will risk leaving behind everything we know in order to seek that which God is building, if we are going to find that which God is doing.

The "gates of hell" are the enemy's access doors into our lives, our congregations, movements, theology, etc. Fear is the primary gate that he uses, just as faith is used as the door for God to have access into our lives. If we are going to walk in the power of God we must have more faith in God to lead us into all truth than we do in the enemy to deceive us. Faith is the door to fellowship with God, because it takes faith to reach beyond the natural realm to the supernatural so that we can "see Him who is unseen."

As we walk in faith that which we start to see with the eyes of our heart starts to become more real to us than what we are seeing with our natural eyes. Then we start living more for the eternal than for the temporary. Those who walk in true faith are naturally going to appear foolish to those who live according to the wisdom of this world, or those who are of a "natural mind."

We take a major step in being delivered from the power of witchcraft when we start to see the Lord so clearly that we serve and respect Him more than anything else; then we are no longer subject to the influence, manipulation and control of those who are still earthly minded, or who move in the power witchcraft.

Those who give themselves to study and become authorities on the nature of evil almost always become darkened and evil in nature themselves. There have been many "cult watchers" who have released a more foul spirit in the church than the cults they were watching—the paranoia they have promulgated has done more to bring division and damage to the church than any cult has been able to do. These have often become the "fault finders" that Jude talked about, printing and distributing slander and gossip as if it were researched fact. As Jude warned, these are being reserved for the "black darkness" (see Jude 10-16), in which many of them have already begun to live.

We do not need to study the darkness as much as we need to study the light. Light is more powerful than darkness. When we open our shades at night darkness does not come in; light shines out into the darkness. Light will always overpower darkness. If we walk in the light we will cast out the darkness. If we walk in the true supernatural power of God we will overpower the evil supernatural power as surely as Moses confounded the sorcerers of Egypt. But Moses would not have been successful had he gone to Egypt with no power, and neither will we if we try to set men free in our own strength. It will take God's power to confront and drive out the increasing power of the enemy.

Most of the cults and New Age groups are now blatantly attacking Christianity and focusing on the church as the primary target of their sorcery. Not only are they infiltrating the church, but they are using most of their power to cast spells and curse those in ministry. What was described in the book *The Harvest* about cult members entering church meetings and performing lewd acts to intimidate and humiliate the church has already begun to happen with alarming frequency.

On the first night of our last conference I went out into the parking lot and found satanic worshipers cursing the meetings. That was a great encouragement to me. They used to come into the meetings! There is no way for Christians to avoid this confrontation, except by growing in spiritual authority to the degree that the enemy will flee from us, and avoid a confrontation at any cost. We are the ones with the power!

Cult groups are wary of attacking those who do have power, so they prey on powerless churches. Their assaults are becoming more bold, and they will continue. God is allowing them to force us to seek Him. The answer for churches which are under this assault is simple—they must seek to know and walk in God's authority and power. He who is in us is much greater than he who is in the world. As the church grows in true spiritual authority the cults are going to start fearing us far more than we do them.

The Power of Cowards—Black Magic

Sorcerers will usually avoid direct confrontation with those who have true spiritual authority because the demons that operate through them rightly fear being humiliated and overcome themselves. These will still attack those who are growing in true spiritual authority and are bearing fruit for the kingdom of God, but they will usually do it secretly. They do this indirectly by sacrificing and cursing according to their black arts.

There is power in satanic sacrifices that we must recognize if we are going to resist it. In II Kings 3:27, the king of Moab offered his oldest son as a burnt offering to his demon gods, and, **"there came great wrath against Israel, and they departed"** (from attacking Moab). It is not biblical for a Christian to fear the enemy, but if we do not understand and properly respect his power, we will be vulnerable to it.

CHAPTER THIRTEEN

The Systematic Attacks of Witchcraft

We need to recognize when we are being cursed with witchcraft so that we can defend against it and shine light into the darkness. Witchcraft operates like hornets who sting their victim over and over until they are killed or driven out. Following are what I call "the stings of witchcraft." These are symptoms that witchcraft is being used against you. Individually, these symptoms may also be attributed to other causes, but if they start to come in this sequence, it is very likely that witchcraft is their source.

Sting 1 — DISCOURAGEMENT. Everyone gets discouraged at times, and it can be for many different reasons. However, if we become subject to growing discouragement for no apparent reason, witchcraft should be considered a possible source. When everything seems to go wrong, the difficulties begin to seem insurmountable and you start to think it is just too hard to go on, even though matters are really not any worse than usual, you are probably coming under spiritual attack. The enemy's main strategy for afflicting you with discouragement is to weaken you for the next level of attack, which is:

Sting 2 — CONFUSION. Again, we must look for a general and pervading "spirit of confusion" for which there is no apparent reason. Here we begin to lose our clarity as to just what we have been called to do, which of course will weaken our resolve. This confusion is meant to compound the discouragement making us even weaker and more vulnerable to further attack, which will usually come in the form of:

Sting 3 — DEPRESSION. This is a deeper problem than simple discouragement; it is an unshakable dread that is the result of both the discouragement and confusion combined, along with a general negligence in spiritual disciplines that has usually slipped in by this time. This leads to:

Sting 4 — LOSS OF VISION. This is the goal of the previous stings and works to increase the effect of all of them. Here we begin to doubt that God has called us to the task in the first place. The only way that we can sail through the storm of confusion is to hold our course. We cannot hold our course if we do not know where we are going. We will not try to hold our course if we begin to question our direction altogether. This will lead to our drifting in circles at the time when we most need to "make straight paths for your feet." This sets us up for the next level of assault:

Sting 5 — DISORIENTATION. This is the combined result of depression, confusion and loss of vision. At this level we have not just forgotten the course we are supposed to be holding, we have even lost our ability to read the compass. The Scriptures will no longer speak to us, we will not trust the Lord's voice and even the most anointed teaching and preaching will seem irrelevant. This is the point of spiritual incapacitation, the inability to function, which results in:

Sting 6 — WITHDRAWAL. This comes when we begin to withdraw or retreat from our purpose in the ministry, from fellowship with the rest of the church, and often from our families and others we are close to. Withdrawal will result in **DESPAIR:**

Sting 7 — DESPAIR. Withdrawal from the battle leads quickly to hopelessness and without hope we can easily be defeated by the enemy, either through temptation, sickness or death. Even science has proven that when hope is removed, often the most healthy person will quickly deteriorate and die. With hope, men and women have lived long past the point when a normal body would have given up. **DESPAIR** will always lead to **DEFEAT.**

In this strategy we can see that the enemy's purpose is to weaken us so that we begin to fall behind; then we can more easily be picked off. In Scripture the Amalekites were typical of Satan and his hordes. It was the practice of the Amalekites to attack the weak and/or defenseless. As the camp of Israel crossed the wilderness, the Amalekites picked off those who fell behind the rest of the camp.

This is why Israel was told that there would be perpetual war with the Amalekites. When Israel's kings were commanded to fight them, they were also commanded to utterly destroy them and not to take any spoil. We have a perpetual war against Satan and we cannot take any prisoners. Neither can we use that which is his in the service of God.

When King Saul disobeyed and kept alive Agag, king of the Amalekites, and kept some of the spoil "in order to sacrifice it to the Lord," it represented a failure of the most foolish kind for any leader of God's people. In those days, keeping a rival king alive after a battle was only done for two reasons: to make him either an ally or a slave. Saul foolishly thought that he could make the one who personified Satan himself either an ally or a slave.

It was no accident that it was an Amalekite who killed Saul and then carried the news of his death to David. This Amalekite thought that the news would be pleasing to David, but David was discerning and had him killed (see II Samuel 1:1-16). If we do not obey the Lord and utterly destroy the enemy we battle, he will end up destroying us. There can be no alliance with the enemy; he must be utterly destroyed. We must not be foolish enough to think that we can use the enemy as our slave; in his guile he will quickly turn the tables.

Witchcraft is being used against the church. Many who have failed to recognize it have been defeated, lost their vision, their ministries, their families and even their lives. This is not sensationalism, it is fact. Paul said that we do not wrestle with flesh and blood, but with principalities and powers (see Ephesians 6:12), and wrestling is the closest form of combat.

The enemy is going to fight; he is going to wrestle with us; if we decide that we just are not going to fight we will get pinned! A Christian has no option as to whether or not he is going to do spiritual warfare if he wants to survive. But how do we combat this witchcraft? We must first look at the basic principle of spiritual warfare required for every victory.

In the book of Revelation, we see that the saints overcome Satan by *1) the blood of the Lamb, 2) the word of their testimony, and 3) loving not their lives even to death* (see Revelation 12:11 KJV). We overcome by the blood of the Lamb as we take our stand on what He has already accomplished for us through the cross. The victory has already been won and there is no way that we can lose, as long as we abide in Him.

The word of our testimony is the Scriptures. Every time the enemy challenged Jesus He simply responded with Scripture, countering the enemy's temptation with God's truth. The Word of God is "the sword of the Spirit"; with it we can ward off the blows from his deceptive words, as well as attack him. Of all the pieces of armor we are commanded to put on (see Ephesians 6:10-18), the sword is the only offensive weapon.

That they "loved not their lives even unto death," reveals the utter commitment to follow Him regardless of the price. We are called to take up our crosses daily, to do all things for the sake of the gospel, to no longer live for ourselves but for Him. To the degree that we remain self centered we will be vulnerable to the enemy's attack.

When we have reckoned ourselves dead to this world, as crucified with Christ, then the enemy no longer has any access to us because he has no more access to Him. If we are dead to this world, what can be done to a dead man? It is impossible for the dead to be offended, to be tempted, to fear, or to be continually looking for the easy way out since he has already paid the ultimate price.

All of these are required for every spiritual victory. Anything less will result in less than a victory. We may make occasional, halting advances, but we will sooner or later be pushed back. But it is clear that at the end of the age there will be an army of God raised up that will not settle for occasional advances—they have committed themselves to the fight and will not stop until there is the complete victory over the enemy that was promised.

It is understood that the total victory will not be accomplished without the personal return of the Lord, but we must fight until He comes, and fight to take every bit of ground that we can, until He appears and takes us up to return with Him and finish the fight. **"The earth is the LORD's, and all it contains" (Psalm 24:1).** Until the earth has been completely recovered from the domain of Satan our fight is not over.

None of us would fight to win if we did not believe that victory was possible. Many teachings have been promulgated in the body of Christ that declare the church's defeat in the end. The whole prophetic testimony of Scripture is that the Lord, the church, and the truth are going to prevail. Satan is being cast down to the earth; he will come with great wrath and there is going to be a time of trouble like the world has never known before—but we will win!

Isaiah 14:16-17 says that when we see Satan we are going to marvel at the pitiful nature of the one who caused so much trouble! He who is in the very least of the saints is much greater than he is, or his antichrists. These times are not to be feared—this is our chance! As Isaiah 60:1-2 declares, when darkness is covering the earth the glory of the Lord is appearing on His people. The darkness will just make His glory upon us appear that much brighter. We must start fighting in order to win, giving no more ground to the enemy and taking back what he's stolen.

To effectively combat witchcraft we must determine that we are going to resist Satan until he flees from us. Our goal is more than just driving the enemy out of our own lives; we then want to pursue him until he is driven out of everyone else in whom he has established a stronghold. The following are some of the ways that we can combat these seven specific areas of Satan's attack through witchcraft.

1) DISCOURAGEMENT. Discouragement *never* comes from God; He is the author of faith and the hope which never disappoints. He does discipline us when we need it, but he never does this by afflicting us with discouragement. **"The wisdom from above is first pure, then peaceable, gentle, reasonable, full of mercy and good fruits, unwavering, without hypocrisy" (James 3:17).** Discouragement is nowhere named as the wisdom that comes from above and it is not a fruit of the Spirit. We must learn to quickly and instinctively reject discouragement and give it no place in our thoughts. We will be led by what we think or feel. We must take every thought captive and make them all obedient to Christ; we must not ever allow discouragement to dictate our course. FAITH is the fruit of the Spirit and the shield of our armor that counters discouragement. If we begin to get discouraged it is because we have dropped our shield. Pick it back up!

2) CONFUSION. Remember that "God is not the author of confusion" and what you are being hit with is not coming from God. In the military, one of the primary elements of battle that a soldier is trained to handle is confusion. There will rarely be a battle when there is not confusion. Very few battles, or projects accomplished, will ever go exactly as planned. The same is true in spiritual warfare. The disciplined soldier who understands this aspect of warfare learns to use the confusion to his own advantage. He does not let it increase his discouragement but begins to anticipate and look for an opportunity to gain an advantage over the enemy. We must learn that confusion is part of the battle and not to be surprised or affected by it. Our resolve to stand and fight will quickly dispel this aspect of the attack.

3) DEPRESSION. God gave to Cain the most effective remedy for depression: **"Then the LORD said to Cain, 'Why are you angry? And why has your countenance fallen [the**

ancient expression for depression]? **If you do well, will not your countenance be lifted up? And if you do not do well, sin is crouching at the door; and its desire is for you, but you must master it' " (Genesis 4:6-7).** Because depression is usually the result of allowing discouragement and confusion to cause us to drift from even our basic spiritual disciplines, such as reading the word, prayer, fellowship, etc., picking them up again with resolve will almost always start to reverse the downward spiral. If we focus on doing what we have been called to do, we will be able to throw off the sin that so easily entangles us.

4) LOSS OF VISION. This attack can also be turned to our advantage and used as an opportunity. When you begin to lose your vision, commit yourself to strengthening your vision. Sink your roots deeper and establish your purpose even more firmly upon the word of God. When God begins to lead us into a purpose we should record how he speaks to us. Review all of the ways that He has led you and search the Scriptures to even more firmly establish His leading.

Above all, hold your course! Do not change your course until you can clearly see the new course. In World War I one of the most effective tactics of the enemy was to lay a smoke screen in front of allied convoys. As the convoy entered the smoke and lost their vision, they would start turning at any perceived sound or whim; the resulting collisions sank more ships than those sunk by enemy torpedoes.

The allies finally developed a simple strategy to overcome this, which will also work for us. When in the smoke every ship was to hold its previous course without deviation. They would soon all sail out the other side into clear air. The same strategy will enable us to more quickly escape what is clouding our vision. When you lose your vision just hold your course and keep going forward.

5) DISORIENTATION. As an instrument flight instructor, the first thing I had to teach a pilot was that, when flying on instruments, his feelings cannot be trusted and must be disregarded. If in instrument conditions, a pilot tries to fly by his feelings, he will quickly lose control of the plane. When you are surrounded by clouds, you can be flying perfectly straight and level but begin to feel like you're turning. If you react to this feeling, you will begin to turn, going off course or maybe even turning the plane upside down.

In a test conducted by the FAA, a group of pilots were flown into instrument conditions without instrument training, and one hundred percent of them lost control of their planes when they tried to rely on their feelings for guidance. I believe that the same is true of Christians who enter spiritual conditions of reduced visibility or "spiritual clouds," and try to rely on their feelings for guidance—they will lose control.

The "instruments" we have been given to walk by are found in the Bible. We do not walk by feelings but by faith in the sure testimony of the word of God. The word of God will keep us oriented and on course if we put our trust in it even though our feelings may be telling us to do otherwise.

6) WITHDRAWAL. In the recent Persian Gulf War, Desert Storm, the majority of casualties were either reserves or civilians. The safest place to be in the war was on the front line. This is also true in spiritual warfare.

When you're being pressed in a battle you cannot call a timeout. On the front line you cannot ask the enemy to stop the battle because you have a headache or want to take a coffee break. On the front line you know the dangers and you do not let your guard down.

Every Christian is on the front line every day whether he likes it or not. Satan will not give you a timeout. It is when we start to consider ourselves a "civilian," or not a soldier, that we will be the most vulnerable to his attack.

Neither is a Christian ever in the reserves. Seldom do battles rage along the entire front for the entire time. There are times of reprieve from conflict, but when you know that you are on the front, even your breaks are taken with vigilance, knowing that a fresh attack can come at anytime. Christians must never take off their spiritual armor and must never lose their vigilance.

There are times and occasions in warfare for strategic retreats. There are times when we overcommit ourselves spiritually and must draw back, but that is not the same as withdrawal from the battle. Even when we have overcommitted ourselves, retreat should be a last resort—an army in retreat is in its most vulnerable condition. If at all possible we should try to at least hold our ground until our position can be strengthened.

We are told to give thanks to God, **"who gives us the victory through our Lord Jesus Christ" (I Corinthians 15:57), "in all these things we overwhelmingly conquer through Him who loved us" (Romans 8:37),** and that He **"always leads us in His triumph in Christ" (II Corinthians 2:14).** Defeat is not an option in Christ. We will gain the victory in that which He has led us to do. The only way that we can be defeated is to quit.

Even when we discover that we have acted presumptuously without being commissioned by God, we do not quit, we repent. There is a difference between quitting and stopping because of repentance. One is a defeat; the other is an adjustment that will always result in further victories. Repentance comes because of the truth that sets us free; defeat will result in a spiritual bondage to the power of the enemy.

7) DESPAIR. The Lord's first observation concerning man was that it was not good for him to be alone. We are social creatures and when we withdraw from fellowship we will usually sink into the deepest pits of hopelessness—despair. At this point in the downward spiral we must return to fellowship and get help in reversing the slide or we will be defeated.

Witchcraft is basically the practice of cursing others. This cursing does not just come through cults or black magic arts, but can even come through those who love us, have good intentions, and are trying to bless us, but are doing it by trying to manipulate us. Witchcraft is rooted in manipulation or a control spirit, regardless of who it comes through.

The mother who manipulates her son or daughter into marrying her choice has done it through witchcraft, and such relationships usually have to be held together through manipulation and control. The prayer group that uses prayers to expose others is gossiping for the sake of manipulation; this is not prayer—it is witchcraft. Much of what is written in the name of Christian journalism as an attempt to keep the church informed is gossip, used for unethical influence or manipulation—this, too, is witchcraft.

Spiritual leaders who use manipulation, hype or control to build their churches or ministries are operating in a counterfeit spiritual authority equivalent to witchcraft. Much of what is taught in business schools is a form of manipulation or control that is witchcraft. Many of the strategies the church has borrowed from secular journalism and the business world have brought witchcraft into the camp, and it must be removed if we are to be free to accomplish our purpose for this hour.

Many of the yokes and human expectations have some power of manipulation and witchcraft attached to them that the enemy has established as a stronghold to conflict with the calling of God in our lives. This is not a license to disregard the expectations of our parents, teachers, employers, etc. We were known by the Lord before we were born, and He placed many of these influences in our lives to help steer us toward our purpose in Him. But some of the yokes and expectations that the well-intentioned parent, teacher or coach puts on us must be cast off. The yokes that are placed on us which are not from the Lord will become clear as we come to know our calling and purpose in Him—the truth will set us free.

The only yoke that we must take is the Lord's yoke. His yoke is easy and His burden is light; and when we embrace it we actually find rest and refreshment instead of pressure and discouragement. These forms of "white" witchcraft can have just as much power as that which comes through black magic arts. The Tree of the Knowledge of Good and Evil has two sides. "White witchcraft" is usually rooted in good intentions but it is the good side of the Tree of Knowledge, whose fruit is just as poisonous as that which comes from the evil side of this tree. White and black witchcraft may be different branches but they have the same root and the same deadly poison.

Those who are unstable will often distort this in order to rebel against God's ordained authority over their lives, receiving the just retribution. King Saul is a personification of one who is ordained by God but fell from his place of true spiritual authority to operate in counterfeit spiritual authority. King David is a personification of true spiritual authority. How did David react to Saul? He was willing to serve the house of Saul until Saul chased him away. Even then he never retaliated, rebelled, or tried to undermine Saul's authority, but honored him as "the Lord's anointed."

Even though David was called to take Saul's place he never lifted his hand against Saul, but determined that if God had really called him then He would have to establish him—he demonstrated the exact opposite of the manipulative or control spirits and by that overcame the evil with good. Had David manipulated his way into the kingdom he would have almost certainly fallen to witchcraft just like Saul. But David was of a different spirit.

Those who are the target of any form of witchcraft will usually feel the stings through the sequence of attacks listed above. If we respond to the attack constructively, we can not only be free of its influence ourselves, but we can also help to free those who operate in witchcraft. The manipulation and control spirits gain entrance through fear. It is the fearful and insecure who become so obsessed with controlling others that they use evil influence and it will take a demonstration of perfect love to cast out these fears. Pray for your attackers to have a revelation of the perfect love of God. Our greatest victory is to win those who are in the enemy's grip, not just to afflict them back.

Blind-siding Yourself

There is another source of witchcraft that can be one of the most unexpected sources of our discouragement, confusion, depression, loss of vision, disorientation and despair—*ourselves!* When we use manipulation, hype or control on others we open ourselves to the consequences.

Before we look at others to find the source we should first look at ourselves. Satan cannot cast out Satan; we will not be able to cast witchcraft out of others if we are ourselves operating in it. Most who have been subject to witchcraft have tried to combat it in the flesh, actually using the same spirit. When we do that it does gain a foothold in our own lives that must be broken before we will have the authority to deliver others.

It is the Father's intent to bring down every form and manifestation of witchcraft operating in the church. It is a serious offense and will not continue to be tolerated. Only after we have been freed from this terrible evil we will also be free to walk in the unprecedented power that can only be entrusted to those who walk in true spiritual authority.

CHAPTER FOURTEEN

The Jezebel Spirit

The spirit of Jezebel usually gains entry when oppression or abuse turns one to bitterness and rebellion. We must keep in mind that God has compassion for the oppressed, and that He even had compassion on the Jezebel in Revelation, giving her "time to repent" (see Revelation 2:21). However, he also rebuked the leaders of that church for tolerating her (see verse 20). We must have compassion on all sinners, but we cannot tolerate their sin.

Those with a Jezebel spirit will attach themselves to almost every anointed church or ministry. Our ultimate goal should always be to see them delivered and healed, but if they do not repent of their ways, they must be removed or they will release everything from continual discouragement and disruptions, to disastrous divisions that will leave many deeply wounded.

First we must identify the Jezebel spirit. The following are characteristics commonly associated with this spirit: Those with a Jezebel spirit will:

1) *continually testify of themselves through their revelation.*

2) *often seek constant recognition; they thrive on being mentioned from the pulpit or by leaders, and may be offended or become distant if they are not.*

3) *try to get close to the leaders, usually through flattery or grand prophecies.*

4) *seldom want to be in authority, but will seek to be "the power behind the throne."*

5) *usually attract the weakest members of the church, and will begin to spiritually enslave them with flattery and/or grand prophecies.*

6) *use their spiritual slaves to spread slander, discontent and division.*

7) *often try to be a matchmaker, and then try to control the relationships that are put together.*

8) *most often have weak spouses (like Ahab), but will proclaim them to be very strong, spiritual, and greatly gifted.*

9) *steal prophecies from others in order to make themselves look better.*

10) *usually feel persecuted.*

11) *often make excuses and never acknowledge their own sins.*

12) *usually be works oriented, often fasting and praying, but with an intent to be considered spiritual.*

13) *often have bitterness, especially toward their father or another male authority figure.*

14) *often have flawed reasoning, which is covered by a pseudo spirituality which implies that only the spiritual can understand them.*

Deliverance from Jezebel

First, we must understand that someone may have one or more of these characteristics but not have a Jezebel spirit. However, if a majority of these do apply to someone you very well may be dealing with this problem. These are all serious flaws that one should be healed or delivered from before he is trusted with a ministry, or with authority in the church.

Some theologians and ministers believe that this spirit was released in the Garden at the time of the fall. If so, it was probably not what caused Eve to be deceived, but could well have been the result of her husband trying to shift the blame on her for the fall (see Genesis 3:12). God gave the command not to eat from the tree to Adam, not to Eve. Though Eve was deceived by the serpent, Adam was the one with the responsibility. Adam was not deceived, he just sinned. Before the fall Eve was his helpmate, it was after the fall that the curse was given to the woman that **"your desire shall be for your husband, and he shall rule over you"** (Genesis 3:16).

The curse of the fall is removed in Christ. This was legally accomplished on the cross, but is a salvation that must be worked out as we are delivered from the consequences of the fall. The original relationship between the man and the woman was not for the man to rule over the woman, or the woman to rule over the man, but for both of them to rule together.

As we are delivered from the consequences of the fall, the closer this relationship should return to the way that it was originally intended. We must never lose sight of our ultimate goal. When we come to fully abide in Christ there is **"neither male nor female"** (Galatians 3:28 KJV).

We must also understand that it is just as much a part of the curse for the man to have to rule over the woman as it is for the woman to be ruled over. Peace and fulfillment will not come to either until they have been delivered from the consequences of the fall and can walk in a right relationship with each other.

There can be a major difference between leading and ruling. One can rule without being a true, gifted leader. A true, gifted leader will not dictate policy as much as lead. However, we know that even Christ will rule over the nations with a rod of iron when He returns, but His bride will be at His side.

In Scripture we can see that a husband was given authority over his wife because of the fall, but nowhere do we see a specific scriptural mandate for authority to be given to women over men, though we do have examples in Scripture where women do have authority. This does not mean that women cannot have authority *with* men. I have three daughters who are prophetically gifted. I learned quickly how specifically the Lord could speak through them. By the time they were three they had my attention when they wanted it. They do not have authority over me, but they do have authority with me.

It is in this same way that the church does not have authority over Christ, and never will, but we do have authority with Him. As His bride, it is His goal for us to rule and reign with Him. His goal is that we will be so one with Him that we will do even greater works on the earth than He did. This should be the same goal of every husband for his wife.

Hope for Jezebel

It is one of the remarkable statements of God's love and grace in all of Scripture that the Lord gave Jezebel "time to repent," even when she was seducing the Lord's people. First, He gave her time to repent because it takes time. This evil gets its roots so deep into a person that it can be one of the longest and most difficult deliverances. However, as deep as Satan has been able to get his roots into a person, that is how deeply they will be filled with the Lord once they are delivered.

Those who are delivered from this spirit can come to know and walk in true spiritual authority on the highest levels. A woman who is delivered from this spirit will become one of the most beautiful and gracious examples of what Eve was really meant to be. A man who is delivered can become a great example of the nobility, dignity and true spiritual authority that Adam was called to be.

Because there is so much excellent material now available about the Jezebel spirit, I will conclude here. My only intent here is to highlight the fact that it is a very significant problem in the church, and we must confront it until it is overcome. Once overcome, it can be a stepping stone to reaching even higher levels of the trust required for the spiritual authority we will need in these last days. Remember that we do not war against flesh and blood. If the Lord could give Jezebel time to repent, we must also, but we must confront her wicked ways or this power will do great damage to the church.

CHAPTER FIFTEEN

The Control Spirit and Legalism

It is one of the basic strategies of the enemy of our souls to enslave the church through "spiritual totalitarianism." This is done by controlling and oppressing believers through fear and intimidation. Fear is the counterpower to faith, and the two are locked in a life and death struggle for every believer. One of the most important battlegrounds for the hearts of men is spiritual slavery versus liberty.

The apostle Paul stated, **"For with the heart man believes, resulting in righteousness" (Romans 10:10).** Fear and intimidation can pressure men into believing with their minds, and even their emotions, but will never change men's hearts. Fear and intimidation used against someone will never result in their having a true faith. Fear is the power of the kingdom of darkness which enslaves. When fear is able to control us, then fear has, in one sense, become our lord. The degree to which faith in God controls us determines His lordship in our lives. Faith is the power of the kingdom of God which sets men free to worship God in Spirit and truth. Fear rules men through external pressure and intimidation. Faith rules from the heart.

A parrot can be taught to say and do the right things, but they will not be in his heart—it is just "parroting." Acceptance which is based on intimidation or pressure will never result in true righteousness or a heart change, regardless of how accurate or true the doctrine is that is being forced upon us. To be true, our faith must come from the heart, not just the mind, because "living waters" can come only from the innermost being, the heart.

We can never really live the truth unless we are able to live from our hearts. We will never be able to teach or preach that which imparts true life until we preach from our hearts where the true living waters abide. In order to be faithful to what is in the heart there must be freedom.

The tendency to associate the "heart" with feelings often causes confusion. Our feelings can come from our hearts, or they can come from other sources which are not our true hearts. Few people, even few Christians really understand their own hearts. Many have so covered their hearts with spiritual or social facades that they are not in touch with what is there. We also have the problem that Jeremiah described, **"The heart is more deceitful than all else, and is desperately sick; who can understand it?" (Jeremiah 17:9).** Even so, it is crucial that we do understand and live by a true heart because that is the only place that true living waters can flow.

One of the ultimate goals of true faith is to change men's hearts, then release them to live by their hearts. Because our hearts are the reservoir of the living waters, when we are freed to live by what is in our hearts, there is a release of the living waters that all men are thirsting for. Christians should be the most free people on earth, and a striking contrast to the rest of humanity. When true Christianity is finally revealed to the world, it will be the greatest light on earth. All men are going to see what they themselves were created to be. This will happen before the end. Why not now? Why not us?

Revival is essentially the release of the living waters within believers. This is why one of the greatest enemies of every revival has been the control spirit. The control spirit enslaves believers and stops the flow of living waters that creates and maintains every revival.

Satan obviously cares very little about what we believe as long as we believe in our minds and not our hearts. In this way truth is used like an inoculation, we are given just enough to appease our consciences, but not enough to change our hearts and bring forth a true faith and a release of living water. Satan's first strategy is to keep religion intellectual. He will give you as much truth as you want as long as he knows you will use it wrongly.

When he sees the truths going beyond the intellectual and reaching hearts, he then sends a control spirit to stop it. The Lord uses truth to set men free, but Satan tries to use truth to bind men, causing them to submit to a control spirit instead of the Holy Spirit.

The Nature of Obedience

The basic conflict between the kingdom of darkness and the kingdom of God concerns slavery and freedom. Jesus said: **"If you abide in My word, then you are truly disciples of Mine; and *you shall know the truth, and the truth shall make you free"* (John 8:31-32).** His truth will make us free as long as we abide in His word, but we must abide in His word. The truth makes us free and freedom is required to comprehend the truth from the heart. Obedience is important to the Lord, but God is not *just* after obedience—He wants us to obey for the right reasons, because we have His heart.

A woman may wear a covering to church as a symbol of her submission to authority. Does wearing that covering make her submissive? Wearing the covering is not the submission, but rather a symbol of it. A rebellious woman may also wear a covering; she may even do it as compensation for her rebellion in an attempt to disguise her lack of submission. The Lord does not ask us to just wear the symbols of our submission—He is looking for submission from the heart. Many of the doctrines promulgated by the church place more emphasis on the wearing of doctrinal "coverings" than on making changes in our hearts. The Lord is not just concerned about *what* we believe, but also *how* we believe.

If all that God required from man was obedience, He would not have given a choice to Adam and Eve in the garden. He could have easily programmed man to always obey, but then He would have only had robots. If there was going to be true obedience from the heart there also had to be the freedom to disobey. That is why the Lord placed the Tree of the Knowledge of Good and Evil in the garden; it was not to cause man to stumble, but it was the place where man could choose to disobey Him. If we are going to have worship in Spirit and truth, worship from the heart, the capability to choose not to worship must also exist.

Worship from the Heart

What good is worship from one incapable of doing otherwise? If our typical "worship services" are an indication of the state of our worship, the Lord might have done just as well to have invented the computer and programmed thousands of them to sing praises to Him. When we are told when to stand, when to sit, what to sing, is any of it coming from our hearts? We may have order, and it may sound good, but is it touching the heart of God? It is difficult to see how it could. Typical church worship, whether it is traditional, Pentecostal, Charismatic, or Third Wave, is usually little more than an attempt to warm up the audience for the main act—the preaching.

We must seek the Lord as to how to attain true worship in our services. Even the most progressive worship quickly gets trapped in spiritual ruts that make it little more than rituals learned by rote, which the Lord said He would never receive as worship. Unless worship enables our hearts to touch the heart of God it is not worship at all—it is just noise. If we touch the heart of God our hearts will be changed. Every worship service should be an encounter with the presence of the Lord. When we behold the glory of the Lord we will be changed by that glory. However, true worship does not come by *trying* to see the Lord, it comes *from* seeing Him.

There are some obvious, practical steps that could be taken to help bring a reality to our worship services. First, why not let the people sit if they want to? If the people have the freedom to sit, when they stand it will be to truly honor the Lord. The "singing in the spirit" that was born (or reborn) during the Welsh Revival, can also be a wonderful format for allowing individuals to truly touch the heart of God with their own worship, as long as it, too, does not just become another ritual. When it is mechanical, or just another tradition, it can become counterproductive, but when believers are released to sing what is in their own hearts to the Lord we have the greatest potential for entering true worship that is in Spirit and truth.

Most congregations do need worship leaders to give some order and direction to a service. The Lord uses leadership in everything, including worship, as we see in the Tabernacle of David and even in the revelations of heaven. But if we are going to touch true worship, there is a point when the worship leader must move out of the way, because as long as we have our attention on the leader we are not really worshipping the Lord from our own hearts; we are following a leader.

I have been in many congregations who did not have a worship leader because they claimed to be led entirely by the Holy Spirit, but were in fact being led more often by the immature and the rebellious. To release a congregation in this effort prematurely can be disastrous, but we should have a vision of maturing to that level. There is a point where true worship can bring such a manifest presence of the Lord that neither the flesh nor the devil will dare to show themselves.

But even if the flesh and the devil do get in from time to time, it may be better to have some wild fires from time to time than to have no fire at all. For there to be the potential for obedience from the heart, God had to give man a choice.

The greater the freedom to choose, the greater the potential for choosing wrongly, and the greater the potential for true heart obedience towards God. When we erect excessive controls, walls and barriers, around our services, programs or doctrines, so that they cannot be disobeyed, then we are only creating spiritual robots who may say and do the right things, but not from their hearts. This is actually counterproductive to producing true Christian faith.

His Sheep Know His Voice

As the apostle taught, **"Now the Lord is the Spirit; and where the Spirit of the Lord is there is liberty" (II Corinthians 3:17 KJV).** If we are going to walk by the Spirit there must be liberty. When we erect a system of rules and regulations to force obedience, we are prohibiting our ability to walk by the Spirit. The New Testament was not meant to be just another Law; it was meant to give us general guidelines while promoting the freedom for us to hear from the Lord ourselves about most issues, even very important ones. The Lord's sheep must know His voice and the freedom of the New Testament is meant to compel each of us to seek Him and to know Him for ourselves.

For example, the Lord does care very much about having His church built according to His own design, but the New Testament is surprisingly ambiguous about both church government and church structure, purposely. This is not so that we can just do whatever we want, but so that we must seek Him and hear from Him to get His instructions. There are some important general principles that we can find as a pattern in the New Testament about church structure, but they are meant to be general so as to promote the need for His builders to each seek Him and hear from Him, because He is the Builder of His house.

The Lord gave us the New Testament to outline some clear general guidelines about life, the church, how we relate to governments, etc., that we must comply with to stay on the path of life. However, these guidelines are general enough to allow for, and promote, liberty. This is not liberty for the sake of license, but so that we would have to seek Him and follow the Holy Spirit in order to be led into "all" truth.

The Lord did not say that when He went away He was going to leave us a book to lead us into all truth, but that He was going to give us His Holy Spirit to lead us into all truth. We should be very thankful for the priceless book that He left to us, but He never meant for it to take the place of the Holy Spirit, or His own place in our life. When it does, it is not just being misused, it has become an idol.

True Christianity is essentially a relationship with Christ, and relationship is essentially communication. As the Lord Jesus affirmed during His own temptation, **"Man shall not live by bread alone, but by every word that** *proceeds* **out of the mouth of God" (Matthew 4:4 KJV).** As we discussed earlier, this is the word that "proceeds," present tense, not that "proceeded," past tense. It is not enough for us to live by what He has said in the past, but we must be hearing from Him today. This is not to imply that this is for the establishing of new doctrines, or to add to the canon of Scripture, but that there is a living, personal relationship that we must all have with Him.

This was the lesson of the manna in the wilderness—it had to be gathered fresh everyday. We, too, must hear from Him everyday—we are called to live by a proceeding word, which reflects a continuing relationship. The quality of every relationship is based on communication. The quality of our faith is based on our communication with the Lord, and the New Testament was meant to promote the liberty that enables, and even requires, each one of us to develop that communication.

Freedom is a prerequisite for a true relationship. If a man forces relations with his wife he is committing rape, not love. The Lord will not rape His bride, the church, but he woos her, causing her to desire submission out of love. It is the evil one who forces and pressures us into obedience or commitments and such will never bring forth true righteousness which can only come from the heart. Manipulation, intimidation and control are not from the Spirit of Truth, but are evil spirits that drive men from the truth and seek to bind them in darkness.

CHAPTER SIXTEEN

The Modern Pharisees

One of the great spiritual battlegrounds of the Reformation was Satan's attempt to keep the Bible out of the hands of the common people. This battle continues to rage today because Satan knows very well that when the "common people" receive the word of God the revolution has begun and that he is about to be overthrown as the prince of this evil age. For this reason the Lord stated as evidence that He was indeed the Messiah, that "the poor have the gospel preached to them."

The Lord does love the poor, but this also has a strategic significance. Present rulers, even spiritual rulers, are usually too comfortable, and too protective of their territory, to respond to the word of God in the radical obedience required to release the living waters from which revival springs. True revival is a revolution. It brings change, and those who are comfortable will always resist change.

This battle to keep the word of God out of the hands of the common people was also raging in Israel when the Lord Himself walked the earth. Interestingly, the Pharisees, who loved and esteemed the Scriptures possibly more than any other sect of their time, were the enemy's main force of arms in this battle. Because of this devotion, they were given the primary responsibility for maintaining the integrity of the Scriptures through centuries of copying and recopying. For this every lover of the Scriptures does owe them much. But in their zeal to protect the Scriptures from abuse, the Pharisees implemented a system of Scriptural interpretation based more on their own tradition than on the actual text.

These traditions caused them to miss, and even persecute, the One who was the personified Word of God—Jesus. Today there are ultraconservative camps in Christianity in which modern Pharisees are doing essentially the same thing that their spiritual counterparts did—in their zeal to protect the Scriptures from doctrinal abuse they have erected a reactionary system of interpretation. This system does in fact protect the Scriptures from the abuse of many who would misinterpret them, but at the same time it works to prohibit those who would radically obey the truth from receiving it.

Everyone who loves the truth wants to have accurate doctrine. However, when we stand before the judgment seat of Christ, we will not be judged on how accurate our doctrines were, but rather by our deeds. Accurate doctrine is not an end in itself, but a means to our being conformed to the image of Christ to better enable us to abide in Him.

Sound doctrine enables us to better determine the will of God so that we can obey Him. But we can have the Bible memorized yet still not know the Truth because Truth is a Person. The Pharisees loved the Scriptures more than they loved the God of the Scriptures, and many today fall prey to this same deception. We cannot love God without loving His word, but we can elevate the written word above Him and make an idol out of the Scriptures, allowing them to supplant our relationship to Him, and to remove the Holy Spirit from the church.

Most believers are not in danger of esteeming the written word too much, but rather of esteeming it too little, and neglecting this priceless gift from the Lord to His people. However, much of this neglect is caused by the ecclesiastical professionals who have imparted such a fear of error that many Christians are afraid to search for truth. At the same time many Christian leaders have esteemed the written word above the living Word and have begun to worship the book of the Lord in place of the Lord of the book. This has caused them to make the New Testament into just another law.

Just as the Pharisees, the greatest lovers of the Scriptures, were the greatest enemy of the Word Himself, some of those who are most outwardly devoted to protecting the integrity of the word are the greatest enemies of the truth today. These modern Pharisees work through fear and intimidation, the arch enemies of truth, just as their spiritual forefathers did. Those who are controlled by fear will be the most threatened by anyone they cannot control through intimidation.

People who believe God with their hearts know the One in whom they believe. When we know that we are known by God, we will not be overly concerned about what anyone else thinks of us. Therefore we will not be threatened or intimidated by anyone on earth. Those with this constitution will make choices based on what is right, not out of political pressures.

False Brethren

Jesus was tolerant of sinners but had little tolerance for the Pharisees and doctors of the law. These were not entering the kingdom and would not allow others to enter either. Modern Pharisees perceive those who have deviated from their inter-pretation of doctrines as enemies, false teachers, or false proph-ets. There are, of course, some false teachers and false prophets. However, the apostle Paul's interpretation of who the real false brethren were is quite different from what is now popularly accepted. He warned against **"false brethren who had sneaked in to spy out our liberty which we have in Christ Jesus, in order to bring us into bondage" (Galatians 2:4).** Those who use fear and intimidation to control others to conform to their beliefs should more often be categorized false teachers than those they so vehemently attack.

Liberty of the Spirit is essential in order to worship "in Spirit and truth." The same battle to infringe on the believer's spiri-tual liberty which raged in the early church is still raging today. If we are going to worship in Spirit and truth, we cannot compromise a believer's freedom to have differences in the nonessential doctrines and beliefs. Those who infringe upon this liberty are the greatest enemies of the truth, even if their stated intent is to protect the truth.

To declare that something is not Scriptural because it is not found in the Scriptures is a wrong application of the Scriptures. The Scriptures were given to free us to do whatever is not specifically banned, not to keep us from doing anything that is not mentioned in them. We must give believers the freedom to do what is not specifically banned in the New Testament, and then judge their fruit as to whether it was of God or not. This freedom does not mean that everything that we do is right; it simply means that in those matters we must seek the Lord individually for His will and His judgment.

There are also times when the Lord would rather us use our own judgment than hear from Him about a matter. As we mature, He would rather us use our own judgment most of the time. If I tell my daughter to witness to one of her friends and she does it, it may please me to a degree, but not nearly as much as if she does it of her own accord.

The first century apostolic teams were not led around by the hand; they were *sent* by God. They used their own judgment most of the time because they had His mind. When the Lord needed to give them special direction, or to change their direction, He gave them a dream, vision, or prophetic word; but by the testimony of the Scriptures, that was in fact rare.

The Lord wants all of His people to know His voice and to have a personal and intimate relationship with Him. All relationships are based on communication, but not all communication is directive. Many people become addicted to prophetic words, which leads to a tragic misuse of the prophetic word. My toddler needs specific and almost continual guidance, but this is not true of my ten year old. As we mature, we should need less guidance, not more. Having to hear from the Lord about every little decision is a sign of immaturity, not maturity.

Prophets are not meant to be gurus. Neither are the Scriptures meant to be used as a horoscope. Even so, for there to be the freedom for believers to know the Lord for themselves, to develop their own relationship to Him, and to know His voice, there must be the freedom for them to also make their own mistakes along the way.

Nothing is impossible with God. It would actually be a small thing for Him to have all Christians believing exactly alike about every doctrine. But true unity of heart will never be attained unless there is a choice not to be unified. Spiritual unity is not based on like doctrines; it is based on love—first for God and then for each other.

By God's design we presently "see through a glass darkly." Each is able to see but a part of the whole picture, and we will never see the whole picture until we learn to put our parts together. God's unity is not a unity of conformity but a unity of many diverse parts. True heart faith is evidenced by tolerance for those who are different, which is required if there is going to be a true unity of the heart.

Each Must Gather His Own Manna

When the children of Israel were given manna from heaven, each household had to gather its own. The same holds true for gathering heavenly manna. We cannot rely solely upon the leaders for our spiritual food. This is not to belittle the importance of leaders and teachers who give themselves to the ministry of the word. Just as the Levites were essential for ministering to the congregation of Israel, our leaders are essential today. But leaders cannot take on the duty of the individual or the individual household. There is a difference between the general teaching that should be provided by those devoted to the ministry of the word, and the daily bread from heaven which must be gathered by each household.

How can an untrained person go to the Bible for a fresh word from heaven without falling into error or false teaching? This is one of the most important issues which has faced God's people during the four thousand years since the written word was first given to man. One of Christianity's greatest struggles has been for the freedom of ordinary people to have access to and interpret the Scriptures for themselves.

Even those movements most devoted to Restoration or Renewal have almost all eventually developed such tight doctrinal statements that they prohibit departure from "the party line." Then they often develop systems and methods of interpreting the Scriptures (hermeneutics) which tend to take this ability out of the hands of the people and keep biblical interpretation solely in the hands of the leaders. Often this can help restrict the misinterpretation and misuse of Scripture, but the very barriers that we erect to protect the Scriptures prohibit further spiritual progress or growth.

Hermeneutical Problems

Most of the hermeneutical systems that have been developed for the noble purpose of trying to prevent heresy or errors also destroy the liberty that is required for a believer to develop his own relationship with the Lord, and worship Him in Spirit and truth. Unfortunately, many of the remedies have too often proven more harmful than the diseases they were designed to treat. This is not a statement against the proper development and use of hermeneutics (hermeneutics is simply a system of interpretation). However, it is a warning against preventing the development of the ability of individuals to read, understand, think and hear from God for themselves.

Both Catholic and Conservative Protestant hermeneutics have been guilty of yoking the people with fear rather than leading people to faith. Like the Pharisees who preceded them, some of the most conservative denominational leaders have erected barriers prohibiting individuals from receiving a fresh revelation or interpretation from the Scriptures. In fact, the very word "fresh revelation" is usually cursed by them with the accusations of men seeking to add to the Scriptures, when this is not what is meant at all. The fresh revelation that is needed is an increased or deeper understanding of the Scriptures. Those who react so strongly to fresh revelation from the Scriptures have erred with one of the most terrible presumptions of all—the belief that they already know all that there is to know.

There are some outstanding hermeneutical principles that can help any sincere seeker of truth to stay on the path that leads to life. Unfortunately, these are often surrounded by many other principles that are designed to protect predetermined interpretations about many non-essential doctrines that are used to limit one's scope, vision, and understanding about almost all biblical teachings.

There is obviously much more to be understood from the Bible than we now understand. Many aspects of conservative hermeneutics prevent, or at least greatly discourage, further exploration and understanding from the Scriptures. This is a tragic and devastating mistake.

With all its different theological camps, the church has become like the proverbial blind men and the elephant. The one who found the leg was sure the elephant was like a tree. The one who found the tail thought that was ridiculous; the elephant was like a rope! The one who found its ear thought that the other two were both mistaken; the thing was like a great leaf. They were all partially right but totally wrong. They could never identify the elephant until they listened to each other and combined their understanding.

The wise psalmist declared, **"The SUM of Thy word is truth" (Psalm 119:160).** Each of us may have a part that is true but it is not the whole *truth* until it is properly fitted together with the other parts of the body of Christ. Understanding and interchanging with the different camps of biblical interpretation can help us to receive the good without stumbling over the bad. Those who know the Spirit of Truth will have the faith in Him to do this. Unfortunately, those who are the most bound by fear, who need the interchange the most, will seldom have the confidence in the Holy Spirit to lead them to the truth. Those who are bound by a control spirit will have more faith in the devil to deceive them than they will have in the Holy Spirit to lead them into all truth.

*There is a God ordained ambiguity preventing the estab-
lishment of an absolute law or method of biblical interpretation.
This ambiguity is designed to keep us dependent on the Holy
Spirit to lead us to truth.* That men would presume that they
could develop a system, or principles, by which they can interpret the Scriptures is in itself an act of profound human arrogance. Such principles try to lay the burden of interpretation
on a science in place of the Holy Spirit. This, in and of itself, is
a departure from the nature of true Christianity—a relationship
with God. If such a thing were possible, why was it not clearly
laid out in the Scriptures, and why do the writers of Scripture
themselves so often depart from these principles?

Certainly there are some principles that can help us in our
quest for biblical truth; but there are no *absolute laws or methods*
of biblical interpretation. When we presume to substitute our
own science for the Holy Spirit, we have by that fallen into
serious error.

The Scriptures contain many paradoxes because the truth is
found in the tension between the extremes. Only the Holy
Spirit can enable us to discern such truth and keep us balanced
between the extremes that divert us from the course. Does this
not open the doors for a great deal of subjectivity in interpreting
the Scriptures? Yes! And that is the point. True Christianity
promotes an extraordinary liberty for the personal quest of
God's truth, a liberty that is required if we are going to believe
from our hearts and not just our minds.

The Highest Form of Unity

When we try to project absolute laws of interpretation, or
doctrines, it may present a semblance of order and unity, but
both the order and the unity will be external, not internal. As
soon as the restraints are removed and we quickly see how
much true order and unity there is; most of the time we will
find chaos. As Martin Luther once quipped, "A spiritual man
does not need a covenant (contract), and an unspiritual man
cannot keep one!"

When we try to get men to comply with our doctrines or commit themselves to our fellowship with human covenants and commitments, we have probably nullified their ability to come into a true unity or a true faith in the doctrine. We have also probably set ourselves up for a future church split.

It is true that we are living in a day of lawlessness. Truth, honor, and the belief that a man's word is his bond is becoming very hard to find. Even so, legalism is not the answer to lawlessness, it only feeds lawlessness, which is why Paul said, **"the power of sin is the Law"** and **"the letter kills, but the Spirit gives life" (I Corinthians 15:56; II Corinthians 3:6).**

When we apply the law to a person, we are only exacerbating the problem by highlighting it without giving the person the grace to overcome it—in this way we make sin manifest. If our constraints are strong enough, we may keep the person under control; but as soon as the restraints are removed he will be even worse. Using the law, we can lock up the criminal; but we cannot change him. As soon as he is released from our prison, he will continue to commit crime because he has not been changed.

Summary

The Lord is seeking truth in the inner man. When we are true in our hearts, we will be true when no one is looking and when no one could find out because truth is in our hearts. When we seek unity by putting external restraints on believers such as covenants and commitments that go beyond the New Covenant that we already have, we are trying to join men to ourselves instead of to Christ; and it will almost always end in a spiritual tragedy.

Men may sincerely desire to keep such covenants when they make them, but all of us are going through the process of change. When we try to hold men to us beyond the time when they want to remain, they may stay longer because of their commitment, but they will ultimately leave. This creates a worse tear in the relationship, and probably more people will be affected by it, because of the guilt and bondage that has been imposed.

The Lord made it easy for His disciples to leave Him and difficult for them to stay. Why would we try to do it differently? Why would we want anyone committed to us if it is not in his heart? Only when a person is free to go, but he continues to stay, do we know that he is really with us in his heart.

When we bind men to ourselves with such covenants it may give us a little more security, but it is a false one. This is putting security in the strength of the bondage that we have brought someone into, not faith in the Lord and what He is building.

To make a covenant is a serious matter, and it can bring us under condemnation if we break it. The New Covenant which we have in Christ, and our marriage covenants, are considered by some to be the only covenants that are biblical. I personally believe that there is a little more liberty than that for making agreements. However, if we are joined to Christ, we are already joined to His body, the church, so why would we need an additional covenant to be joined to anyone spiritually?

When we are compelled to make covenants with people, local congregations, or movements, it is a covenant that is outside of the New Testament; and both the New Testament and history testifies that it is likely to end badly. When Peter made the commitment that he would never deny the Lord, he could not even keep it through the night.

I have heard some very eloquent and moving messages about the beauty of David and Jonathan's covenant, but the tragic ending to that relationship is a poignant example of this point—Jonathan still died in the house of Saul although he had committed himself to the house of David. However, we must also appreciate David's heart to keep the covenant even with Jonathan's children. A noble soul will keep his agreements even when the other party does not.

Why should we put people under unnecessary pressure to be joined to us or our work? This only reflects the shallowness of our leadership and the lack of the Lord's presence. When the Lord Jesus is lifted up, all men are going to be drawn to Him; and we do not need any other props. When we try to lift up ourselves or our works in His place, which is what we are doing when we pressure men to commit to us or to our work, they will inevitably become disappointed and be scattered, with great injury to all.

The first council in Jerusalem resulted in the most important declarations in church history, and they established a biblical liberty for all Christians. After contending with the believers from the sect of the Pharisees, who had been compelling the young church to continue keeping the Law of Moses, the apostles and elders stated,

For it seemed good to the Holy Spirit and to us to lay upon you no greater burden than these essentials: that you abstain from things sacrificed to idols and from blood and from things strangled and from fornication; if you keep yourselves free from such things, you will do well. Farewell (Acts 15:28-29).

Does this mean that we can do anything else, watch anything we want on television, look at pornography, gamble, etc.? Of course not. It means that we are all required to be led by the Holy Spirit and to obey Him. It means that we learn to walk by the "perfect law of love." If we love the Lord, our families, the church, and our neighbors, we would not do those things that could hurt them, or waste our time with such trivia when we could be spending it with them.

The control spirit, which is often manifested through human covenants or the use of guilt and pressure, is the manifestation of counterfeit spiritual authority. We only have true spiritual authority to the degree that Jesus lives within us. When He lives within us, we are acutely aware that He is building His church, and that He is quite able to do it perfectly. Therefore, we can relax.

When we minister in true spiritual authority we are yoked with Him, which means He is going to be the one pulling the weight—His yoke really is easy and His burden is light. When we take it, we really do find rest for our souls. We only have to strive when we are building in our own strength.

Liberty is essential for a true Christian walk. Increasing liberty should always be our goal, but it must be understood that increasing liberty is relative to increasing maturity. I cannot give my three year old nearly the liberty that I give my ten year old. Obviously, new believers generally need much more supervision and help than more mature Christians. The real issue is: are we promoting spiritual liberty and truth that will change men's hearts, that is not based on human constraints and pressures to get men to conform? We will never have true worship from the heart if we do not have freedom.

CHAPTER SEVENTEEN

Our Greatest Power and Our Greatest Enemy

There are two ministries which go on continually before the throne of God: one is the ministry of *intercession*, the other is *accusation*. Jesus "lives to intercede" for His people. To the degree that we abide in Him, Jesus will use us to intercede; His church is to be a "house of prayer for all the peoples." Satan is called "the accuser of the brethren" and we are told that this ministry goes on "day and night before the throne of God" (see Revelation 12:10). To the degree that the enemy has access in our life he will use us to accuse and criticize. Like the two trees in the garden, we must all choose which of these ministries we are going to embrace.

We may ask how Satan could continue to accuse the saints before God if he has been thrown out of heaven and no longer has access to the throne? The answer is that Satan uses the saints, who do have access to the throne, to do this diabolical work for him. Satan is called by many titles but certainly his most effective guise has been "the accuser of the brethren." This title was given to Satan because of his effectiveness in getting brother to turn against brother. Causing division is his specialty. His greatest victory over the church is turning the brethren against each other; *accusation* has been his most effective and deadly tool in destroying the light, the power and the witness of the body of Christ.

The greatest threat to Satan's domain is the unity of the church. The devil knows very well the authority Jesus has given to any two that will agree. He knows that with agreement between just two saints the Father will give them what they ask. He understands that one saint can put a thousand to flight but two of them together can put ten thousand to flight. Unity does not just increase our spiritual authority—it multiplies it exponentially.

Ironically, the access the accuser has to most of us is through our insecurity, which drives us to become territorial. The insecure are threatened by anything which they cannot control. We may use doctrines or a feigned noble determination to protect the truth or the sheep, but I have never witnessed a division in the church which was not rooted in territorial preservation.

The resulting divisions that we cause while trying to protect our domains in fact cuts off our true spiritual authority and anointing. This ultimately results in our losing the very thing we are trying so desperately to preserve. It is an incontrovertible law of the spirit, if you seek to save your life you will lose it. If you will lose your life for the Lord's sake you will find it. Isaiah addressed this issue most succinctly in chapter 58:

> **Then your light will break out like the dawn, and your recovery will speedily spring forth; and your righteousness will go before you; the glory of the LORD will be your rear guard.**
> **Then you will call, and the LORD will answer; you will cry, and He will say, "Here I am." *IF* you remove the yoke from your midst, the pointing of the finger, and speaking wickedness (verses 8-9).**

Do you need more light in your life? Do you wonder why recovery and healing do not come? Why do troubles tend to follow you more than the glory of the Lord? You call to the Lord but He does not answer; you even cry out to Him but cannot find Him. The reason for this is almost always the same—we have a yoke in our midst called **"the pointing of the finger, and speaking wickedness"**—which is a critical spirit. He promised through Isaiah that our lives could radically change when we remove that yoke. As the wise Solomon observed:

But the path of the just is like the shining sun, that shines ever brighter unto the perfect day.

The way of the wicked is like darkness; they do not know what makes them stumble (Proverbs 4:18-19 NKJV).

If we are walking in righteousness we will be walking in increasing light. It is true that those who stumble around in the dark seldom know the reason for that darkness or they would not be in it. The critical person is usually critical of everyone but himself. As the Lord stated, he is so busy looking for specks in the eyes of his brothers that he cannot see the big log in his own eye, which is the reason for the blindness.

When we criticize another brother or sister, we are actually saying that God's workmanship does not meet up to our standards, that we could have done it better. Which one of us can even make ourselves into what we should be? If we cannot even make ourselves how will we make someone else? When we criticize someone else's children, who will take offense? The parents! This is no less true with God. When we judge one of His people we are really judging Him. When we judge one of His leaders we are really judging His leadership; we are by that saying that He does not know what He is doing with the leadership He is providing.

Such grumbling and complaining is the same problem that kept the first generation of the children of Israel from possessing their promised land. Their grumbling caused them to spend their entire life wandering in dry places. This is the chief reason why so many Christians do not walk in the promises of God; instead they spend their lives in the wilderness going around the same mountains (problems) over and over again. As we have been warned:

Do not speak evil of one another, brethren. He who speaks evil of a brother and judges his brother, speaks

evil of the law and judges the law. But if you judge the law, you are not a doer of the law but a judge.

There is one Lawgiver, who is able to save and to destroy. [When we judge the law we judge the Lawgiver.] Who are you to judge another? (James 4:11-12 NKJV).

When we "point the finger" to criticize we yoke ourselves. The Lord warned us:

Judge not, that you be not judged.

For with what judgment you judge, you will be judged; and with the measure you use, it will be measured back to you (Matthew 7:1-2 NKJV).

The Spirit of Poverty

I once visited a state that was under the most powerful spirit of poverty I have witnessed in this country. One characteristic which stood out concerning the nature of the people there was how they would scorn and criticize the wealthy, or anyone who was just doing well. By this these people had yoked themselves with their own judgments so that they could not be blessed.

We may sometimes be called to be abased, and sometimes we need to abound. The apostle Paul even claimed to have gone hungry at times, and he sternly warned us to be content if we just have food and covering (see I Timothy 6:8). Even so, if I am to be abased I want to do it in submission to God and to what He is trying to work in my life, not in submission to an evil spirit of poverty. I certainly do not want to be yoked to poverty because of my own judgments of others.

In that state many of the pastors I met had actually yoked themselves and their congregations to poverty by criticizing how other men of God took up offerings. Because of their judgments they could not even take up a biblical offering without feeling guilt. As they had sown suspicion about those who spent too much time taking up offerings, their own people began to suspect them if they took any time. As their judgments came back upon them they only knew darkness and unanswered prayer with regard to their needs.

What is true with regard to finances can also be true with regard to spiritual gifts. I met in that state many who had significant mantles of spiritual authority, who should have had national or international influence in the church, but spent their lives ministering with little fruit to shrinking churches.

Sometimes our crowds will shrink because we are doing the right thing, just as the Lord's own departed when He preached things hard for them to receive, but this was not the case with these men. They had judged and criticized the ministries of others who were gaining influence and had thereby yoked themselves. God could not give them the platform which would have produced the fruit their anointing and authority should have produced. Our criticisms will bring us to poverty. **"Death and life are in the power of the tongue, and those who love it will eat its fruit" (Proverbs 18:21).**

Criticism is one of the ultimate manifestations of pride because it assumes superiority. Pride brings that which any rational human being should fear the most—*God's resistance.* **"God resists the proud, but gives grace to the humble" (James 4:6).** We would be better off having all of the demons in hell resisting us than we would be having God stand against us.

Truth Can Kill

Our criticisms can be rooted in true discernment. The ones we criticize may well be in error. These pastors who criticized the way others raised money through manipulation, hype and sometimes outright deception, were accurate. We must walk in discernment, and the apostle made this plain, saying, **"do we not judge those who are within the church?"** *The issue is how we deal with what we discern: are we going to use it to accuse or to intercede?* Which ministry are we going to be a part of? How we deal with discernment can determine the outcome of our own spiritual lives.

A worthless person, a wicked man, walks with a perverse mouth;

he winks with his eyes, he shuffles his feet, he points with his fingers;

perversity is in his heart, he devises evil continually; he sows discord.

Therefore his calamity shall come suddenly; suddenly he shall be broken without remedy (Proverbs 6:12-15 NKJV).

The very last thing the Lord indicated that we ever want to be is a stumbling block; it would be better for us to not even be born than to cause even one of His little ones to stumble. In Matthew chapter 18, He gave clear instructions about how we are to deal with a brother who is in sin. He did this to keep us from becoming stumbling blocks.

First, we go to him *in private*. Only after he has rejected our counsel do we go to him with another brother. Only after he has rejected both should we ever go before the rest of the church with the issue. If we do not follow this pattern we will be in jeopardy of becoming the last thing we ever want to become—a person who has caused one, for whom our Lord gave His own life, to stumble.

I have heard numerous excuses for not following Matthew 18 in bringing correction. A popular one is: "I knew they would not listen to me." I have also heard the excuse, "If they have a public ministry we have a right to expose them publicly." This is quite preposterous because every ministry is public, at least to a degree. Who determines the degree to which it has become public that frees us from compliance with God's word? The Lord gave no such conditions.

Those who take such liberties with the clear commandments given by Jesus Himself are by this claiming to have authority to add to the word of God. If a man we believe is in sin has a large ministry and is inaccessible to us, we can conclude that we must not be the one called to bring the judgment. In such a case, we should not accuse—we should intercede. The Lord is able to judge His own house and He is able to make a way for us if we are the ones He wants to use. If He does not make a way for us, we can trust Him to do it in His own time. Again, this is to protect us from coming under a judgment that is more severe than the brother who is in sin.

If we have not followed the Lord's prescribed manner for dealing with a brother who is in sin, we have absolutely no right to talk about it to anyone else, much less to go public with it. It should not even be shared to get another's opinion on the matter. What we may call getting someone else's opinion, God calls gossip. He is not fooled and we will pay the price for such indiscretions.

His commandment was to first go to the person in private. Only after we have done that should we talk to another person, and then only for the purpose of going to help the one in sin. Our goal must always be to deliver the brother out of his sin, not just to expose him. Paul warned, **"Brethren, if a man is overtaken in any trespass, you who are spiritual restore such a one in a spirit of gentleness, *considering yourself lest you also be tempted*" (Galatians 6:1 NKJV).**

Love Covers

Let us not succumb to pettiness in our challenges concerning another's sin. **"Love covers a multitude of sins" (I Peter 4:8).** The majority of us still have a few hundred things wrong in our lives that the Lord is not finished with. He is usually dealing with one or two of them at a time because that is all we can handle. It is one of Satan's strategies to try and distract us into trying to deal with the other three hundred problems we have, resulting in frustration and defeat.

Matthew 18 was not given to us to use as a club for letting our brother know how he offended us. If we have love we will cover most of those unless it is bringing unnecessary injury to our brother. We must use this Scripture, and indeed all Scripture, in love, not out of self-preservation or in retaliation.

Of course, the Lord Jesus Himself is our perfect model. When He corrected the seven churches in Revelation, He gave us a perfect model for bringing correction in the church. He first praised each church and highlighted what they were doing right. He then straightforwardly addressed their problems. Incredibly, He even gave Jezebel an opportunity to repent! He then gave each church a wonderful promise of reward for overcoming their problems. The Lord never changes. When He brings correction today it always comes wrapped in encouragement, hope and promises.

The "accuser of the brethren" is also trying to bring correction to the church. His methods and his goals are obviously quite different. Jesus encourages and gives hope; Satan condemns and tries to impart hopelessness. Jesus builds one up so that they can handle the correction; Satan tears you down trying to get you to quit. Jesus loves us and wants to bring us to the highest place that He can. Satan's goal is destruction.

One of the more remarkable phenomenon of the Pentecostal and Charismatic movements has been the inability of those inclined to spiritual gifts and experiences to discern the spirits. There seems to be the least discernment of the most deadly enemy spirit of all—the accuser of the brethren! Could it be that our judgments against those who do not have the baptism, or other spiritual experiences like ours, have yoked us with an inability to discern the spirits? Even without the spiritual gift of discernment, James gave us clear guidelines for discerning the source of wisdom, which if we had heeded would have preserved the church from some of her most humiliating failures:

Who is wise and understanding among you? Let him show by good conduct that his works are done in the meekness of wisdom.

But if you have bitter envy and self-seeking in your hearts, do not boast and lie against the truth.

This wisdom does not descend from above, but is earthly, sensual, demonic.

For where envy and self-seeking exist, confusion and every evil thing are there.

But the wisdom that is from above is first pure, then peaceable, gentle, willing to yield, full of mercy and good fruits, without partiality and without hypocrisy.

Now the fruit of righteousness is sown in peace by those who make peace (James 3:13-18 NKJV).

We are saved by grace and we need all of the grace that we can get to make it through this life. If we want to receive grace, we had better learn to give grace because we are going to reap what we sow. If we expect to receive mercy, we had better start sowing mercy, and most of us are going to need all of the mercy we can get. The very last thing that we want to do is come before the Lord on that day with our brother's blood on our hands. He warned,

You have heard that it was said to those of old, "You shall not murder, and whoever murders will be in danger of the judgment."

But I say to you that whoever is angry with his brother without a cause shall be in danger of the judgment. And whoever says to his brother, "Raca [Empty head]!" shall be in danger of the council. But whoever says, "You fool!" shall be in danger of hell fire.

Therefore if you bring your gift to the altar, and there remember that your brother has something against you,

> leave your gift there before the altar, and go your
> way. First be reconciled to your brother, and then
> come and offer your gift.
> Agree with your adversary quickly, while you are
> on the way with him, lest your adversary deliver you
> to the judge, the judge hand you over to the officer,
> and you be thrown into prison [bondage].
> Assuredly, I say to you, you will by no means get out
> of there till you have paid the last penny (Matthew
> 5:21-26 NKJV).

The context of this warning is that, if we have been guilty of
slandering a brother, we should forget about our offerings to
the Lord until we have been reconciled to our brother. We often
think that our sacrifices and offerings can compensate for such
sins but they never will. We will stay in the prisons we make for
ourselves with our judgments until we have paid the last cent,
or until we are reconciled to the brother we slandered.

The Lord said that when He returned He was going to judge
between the sheep and the goats (see Matthew 25:31-46).
Those who are judged to be sheep inherit the kingdom and
eternal life. Those who are designated as goats are sent to eternal
judgment. The separation was determined by how each group
had treated the Lord, which was reflected in how they had
treated his people. As John stated:

> If someone says, "I love God," and hates his
> brother, he is a liar; for the one who does not love his
> brother whom he has seen, cannot love God whom
> he has not seen (I John 4:20 NIV).

> Everyone who hates his brother is a murderer; and
> you know that no murderer has eternal life abiding
> in him.

We know love by this, that He laid down his life for us; and we ought to lay down our lives for the brethren (I John 3:15-16).

One of the great tragedies of church history has been the way leaders of each move of God have become opposers and persecutors of succeeding moves. To date this trend has not failed. Numerous leaders have spent their lives serving faithfully and well, only to end as vessels for the accuser, who makes them a stumbling block for the next move.

As a new move of the Spirit is now this terrible separation between spiritual generations has again begun to appear. As we forewarned our readers in January of 1989 (in the article *An Onslaught Against the Church*), "the accuser of the brethren" has been released with unprecedented rage. Satan's highest goal is to get brethren accusing and dividing against one another.

The Lord is allowing this onslaught in order to purify His church, and to work humility into many of those He is about to release with increasing power and authority. He is also allowing the accuser to surface in the church so that He can cut his head off. The Lord will vindicate those who are falsely accused in a way that will put a holy and pure fear of the Lord in His people so that we will not continue to give dominion in our hearts to the accuser.

What is it that causes leaders of one move to become opposers of the next move? There are several factors involved, which we must understand and be delivered from or we will end up repeating the same error. We may think and say that we would never do this, but that is what everyone has thought and said who has ended up doing it. **"Therefore let him who thinks he stands take heed lest he fall" (I Corinthians 10:12).** The pride that causes us to assume we will not do it is one of the very factors that leads to our fall.

This problem actually precedes church history and goes all the way back to the very first two brothers born into this world.

The older could not bear the younger because, as John observed:

> **For this is the message which you have heard from the beginning, that we should love one another;**
> *not as Cain, who was of the evil one, and slew his brother. And for what reason did he slay him? Because his deeds were evil, and his brother's were righteous* **(I John 3:11-12).**

Each move of the Holy Spirit has resulted in the restoration of more light to the church. This is not new truth but truth that was lost by the church through the Dark Ages of her history. Regardless of what we call our opposition, a basic reason for most of it is jealousy. Those in leadership, or who have been faithful to the light they have for a time, cannot believe the Lord would use anyone but them for further restoration of His truth and purposes.

Men with natural leadership abilities are usually those who attain the greatest positions of influence in the church. These are not wimps, and it is difficult for them to give up leadership. Even so, if we lean on our natural leadership abilities, instead of simply obeying the Lord, we will almost certainly be doomed to the ultimate failure of becoming a stumbling block.

True spiritual leadership is rooted in the humility of servanthood, not in natural abilities. The more the apostle Paul grew in true spiritual authority the more determined he became to **"put no confidence in the flesh,"** but to **"glory in his weaknesses."** It is only those domains that we, ourselves, have established that we will have to protect. Those who truly have their authority established by God trust God to keep that which has been entrusted to them.

The only remedy leaders have to keep from falling to this terrible trap is to seek the humility and nature of John the Baptist. This man is one of the greatest types of true spiritual ministry. His whole purpose in this life was to prepare the way for Jesus, to point to Him, then to decrease as the greater One increased. John's joy was to see the bridegroom's joy.

True spiritual leaders must have the attitude of "spiritual" eunuchs. A eunuch's whole purpose was to prepare the bride for the king. It was not even possible for the eunuch to desire the bride, but his whole joy was in his king's joy. Jesus "emptied Himself and became of no reputation, taking the form of a bond servant." So must all who would walk in true spiritual authority. When we use the ministry in order to make a reputation, to find those who will serve us and to be filled ourselves, we will not have the authority of Christ.

It is not always the older generation of leadership that has been the stumbling block; the new generation has been just as guilty of causing the previous one to stumble! The very arrogance of presuming that we are the new generation (in contrast to the old) is rooted in a pride that God has to resist. This is a humiliating slap in the face to men and women who have given their lives to faithfully serving the Lord and His people.

Jesus did not ridicule John the Baptist for being a part of the old order—He honored him. Jesus even submitted Himself to John's ministry. This submission did not entail allowing John to control Him, but He acknowledged John and esteemed him and his work.

Why is it that abused children grow up to be abusers? Why is it that accused saints grow up to become accusers? The answer is the same for both. Abused children usually grow up judging their parents and determined not to be like them. So they become reactionary, which does not lead to grace but feeds and nurtures the bitterness—which ultimately results in their becoming just like their parents. Only humility, repentance and forgiveness will ever break that cycle. The sins of the parents will become the sins of the children until we receive the grace of the cross. God gives His grace to the humble—those who understand that they *will* be like their parents without His help.

There will be a generation that will be persecuted like every one before it, but which will not go on to persecute the next move. This movement will not have become subject to the "pride of generations," assuming that all things will be concluded with them. This generation will have found the grace of the cross, having forgiven from the heart those who mistreated them.

This generation will also perceive and even hope that their children, spiritual and natural, may go further in Christ than they went and will rejoice in it. They will give their lives to making the way of that generation as smooth as possible, and will then rejoice to decrease as that generation arises. They will be of the spirit of Elijah who will return the hearts of the fathers to the sons, and the hearts of the sons to the fathers.

Our ability to be such a generation, which prepares the way for the Lord and His ultimate purposes, will be determined by which of the two ministries we choose—accusation or intercession. Let us now remove the terrible yoke of "pointing the finger" from our midst and begin turning our criticisms into intercession.

Then your light will break out like the dawn, and your recovery will speedily spring forth; and your righteousness will go before you; the glory of the LORD will be your rear guard.

Then you will call, and the LORD will answer; you will cry, and He will say, "Here I am."

And the LORD will continually guide you, and satisfy your desire in scorched places, and give strength to your bones; and you will be like a watered garden, and like a spring of water whose waters do not fail.

And those from among you will rebuild the ancient ruins; and you will raise up the age-old foundations; and you will be called the repairer of the breach, the restorer of the streets in which to dwell (Isaiah 58:8-9, 11-12).

PART III

The Victory

CHAPTER EIGHTEEN

The Quest

Behold, I stand at the door and knock; if any one hears My voice and opens the door, I will come in to him, and will dine with him, and he with Me (Revelation 3:20).

This Scripture presents a great dilemma for every seeker of God. Here we see the Lord on the outside knocking, seeking to gain entrance into His own church. This should raise several important questions: Why would Almighty God knock on the door to be let in to His own church? Why does He not just enter? Why is He on the outside? What are the knocks that He is using to get our attention so that we will open the door?

We also know that when the Lord returns He is not going to be so patient with the heathen. He is coming to rule with a rod of iron. The Lord could have begun such a rule immediately after His resurrection, but He had another, higher purpose.

The entire church age has existed for the purpose of calling those who would rule and reign with Him. The primary purpose for the church age has been the formation of the church, not the reformation of the world. He has been completing His church in the heavenly places, made up of the overcomers in each generation. That is why His call to the Seven Churches in Revelation were to the overcomers. Their influence on the earth has brought reform as they have been the salt of the earth, but when the Lord Himself returns with them, the world will be changed, and will become obedient to Him. Even so, after the transformation is complete we see that Satan is released again for a short time in order to prove that their obedience is from the heart.

It may seem contradictory, but for obedience to be from our heart it must *not* be our primary objective. The greatest commandment is to love the Lord, not to obey Him, because if we do not obey Him out of love our obedience will not be from our hearts. Love finds, as its conclusion, obedience; but obedience does not necessarily originate in love. If we esteem love above obedience we will obey Him better than if we esteem obedience above love. Obedience can actually become an idol that separates us from God. This will then quickly lead to our serving in a religious spirit, which seeks to have us base our relationship to God on performance rather than grace.

This is not to negate the importance of obedience, leadership or structure in our churches and ministries. Leadership and organization are not automatically in conflict with the Holy Spirit. The highest form of worship usually does not come just because we are open for anything, but rather because we have sought the Lord and know ahead of time what He wants to do, and plan accordingly.

The Plan

It is not possible to share a word like this without there being a danger of overreaction on the part of some. For example, many who begin to see the freedom that we must have to walk with God, can develop a belief that it is impossible to follow the Holy Spirit if we have any predetermined plans or agendas. Such a mentality is often more in harmony with the spirit of lawlessness than with the Holy Spirit.

Consider the example of the order that is found in nature; it is not the result of a lack of planning, but of the longest range planning possible—God planned what we are now doing before the foundation of the world! If we are in harmony with the Holy Spirit we, too, should be able to see much farther ahead, and be able to plan accordingly. Planning is a basic part of God's nature, and should be ours, too.

This does not mean that we should be ruled by planning committees, but He wants to give us His plans. When Moses was commissioned to build a dwelling place for the Lord, He gave him specific, detailed plans for it. We, too, must learn to go up on the mountain into His presence to receive our plans from Him. If all who are called to be builders would receive their plans from Him, instead of just copying each other's plans, there would be a great deal more diversity and life in the body of Christ.

The liberty of the Spirit should never be interpreted as license to do whatever we want to do. The true liberty of the Spirit is the freedom to follow the Spirit. Some congregations may actually be too free, allowing almost anything out of a fear of missing the Holy Spirit. I have sat through many meetings that were supposedly "led by the Spirit," but were in fact led more by the immature, the unstable, and the rebellious, who quickly filled the void left by the lack of leadership. The fact is that the Holy Spirit is rarely able to do anything in such meetings, or through churches or movements that lack strong decisive leadership.

Peter warned that the "unstable and untaught" were distorting the words of Paul, as well as the rest of the Scriptures, to their own destruction (see II Peter 3:16). We will always have the unstable and untaught among us who will try to dictate the course to their own liking and comfort. To allow them to do this is to be led into the same destruction that they are headed for. The Lord's goal is not to bring us to a place of no leadership in the church, but where the leadership is more fully joined to Him. One of the ultimate conflicts at the end of the age will be with the spirit of lawlessness, and we must not allow it to have its way in the church.

Being "open to the Holy Spirit" does not mean that we walk around perpetually not knowing what to do next, which will only lead to serious instability. Being open to the Spirit does mean that we must always be open to changes, but only to the changes that He wants to make. The Lord Jesus did not go through life never knowing what the Spirit was going to lead Him to do. He always knew what the Spirit was leading Him to do next. That is how He is calling us to walk. The true freedom of the Spirit comes from knowing clearly what we are called to do, which releases us to go forward with boldness.

There is probably far more evil released and tolerated through the lack of planning than there is through wrong planning. There is truth to the proverb that, "Those who fail to plan, plan to fail." But our goal must be to plan by the Spirit rather than according to mere human wisdom. It is not wrong to plan worship, or other things that we are called to do. The point of stumbling comes when we try to use the plan as the motivator rather than our love for the Lord.

In worship it is not enough to just do the right things—we must do them for the right reasons. Worship, or obedience, that is performed out of compulsion, or hype, can be a deception by which we appease our consciences. At this point, we are no longer compelled to seek the reality. Jeremiah wrote:

My people have become lost sheep; their shepherds have led them astray. They have made them turn aside on the mountains; they have gone along from mountain to hill and have forgotten their resting place (Jeremiah 50:6).

Early in my ministry the Lord showed me that I was one of those shepherds who was leading His sheep astray. I was doing it in this same way; leading the people from one high place to the next, from project to project, hype to hype, always keeping them moving and trying to keep them excited, but not leading them to their resting place—an intimate relationship with the Lord Himself. This is possibly the primary reason for the Laodicean spirit of lukewarmness in the church today—she is simply weary of going from project to project but never really connecting to the Lord. We "lead people to the Lord," but somehow all they ever get is us!

God's Second Book

True worship contains diversity. God's diversity is much more profound than just changing the songs we sing. Jon Amos Comenius called nature "God's second book." This was essentially what Paul said in Romans 1:20: **"For since the creation of the world His invisible attributes, His eternal power**

and divine nature, have been clearly seen, being understood through what has been made, so that they are without excuse."

Everything that was made reflects the Creator. The awesome diversity of the creation reflects one of the basic attributes of our Creator—He is creative! He makes every snowflake different. There are no two trees in the world exactly alike. He made every human being unique and different. If this is such a basic characteristic of His creation, why is it that the church, which is supposed to be the embodiment of His nature and ways, is so boringly uniform?

Why is it that we try to make every congregation alike? Why do our church meetings tend to always follow the same pattern? How is the church, supposedly the dwelling place of our glorious Creator, so devoid of creativity? Possibly the greatest threat to the church today is not persecution from liberals, or even sin, but terminal boredom. What we often call church planting is nothing more than franchising, which may have more in common with Burger King than the King of kings. Mistaking uniformity for obedience may well prove to have been one of the church's most devastating mistakes.

We claim that God is a God of order, and He is, but His order is very different from our typical human concept of order. The basic human concept of order is uniformity. We like straight rows, singing in harmony, everyone in the choir wearing the same color robes, and everything else very neat and tidy. However, if you really want to see God's order take a walk through the woods. There are no straight lines in nature. There seems to be no system to the way all kinds of different trees and plants grow up right next to each other. It looks like chaos, but there is an order in nature that is so intricate that no human mind has yet fathomed it. What looks to the human mind as chaos is, in fact, an order and harmony far beyond our comprehension.

Having our chairs in straight rows and a devotion to neatness is not necessarily contrary to God's order. In most cases it is just practical. Even so, we must understand that this in itself does not reflect God's order. The Lord Jesus, who was in perfect obedience to the Father, never seemed to do anything the same way twice. He healed many different people, but almost every time He used a new method.

Both the Lord's messages and the settings in which He gave them changed daily. He was so diverse in His ministry that John finally wrote that if everything that He did had been written that even the world itself could not have contained the books. How is it that the people who are supposed to be conformed to the image of the Prince of Life are so lifeless, void of creativity, and predictable?

The *New* Covenant

One of the primary reasons for this bondage to uniformity in the church has been the subtle theology promoted by many which essentially teaches that the New Testament is just another law. The New Covenant was not given to be another law, but to free us from the yoke of the law. The New Testament was not given to restrain us from doing anything that was not specifically written in it, but rather to free us to do whatever is not directly forbidden by it. There is a fundamental difference in these two approaches which is nothing less than the same conflict that existed in the Garden through the two trees placed there. **"For the letter kills, but the Spirit gives life" (II Corinthians 3:6).**

Only when there is true liberty can there ever be true unity. True unity is not found just in uniformity. The only place where we can now find unity in uniformity among men is in the cemetery! The closer we are to that ideal of unity the closer to being dead we are. Francis Frangipane likes to say, "True Christianity is not following a manual, but rather following Emmanuel." True Christianity is a reunion and relationship with our blessed Creator, not just learning to follow a book of procedure. The Scriptures give us general guidelines that keep us safe, but also are broad enough to free us to each seek Him, and to relate to Him in a unique and special relationship.

The Unholy War

It is true that those who fail to esteem the Scriptures will end up just as deceived, and probably more demented and perverted, than those who wrongly replace the Holy Spirit with the Scriptures. If we had to choose one form of deception I would choose the one that esteemed the Scriptures beyond their designated purpose, but the path that leads to life is not found in either of these extremes. One extreme will lead to our death by the letter that kills. The other extreme leaves us dead in our transgressions.

As the Lord explained, **"You do err not knowing the Scriptures or the power of God" (Matthew 22:29 KJV).** Presently, those who know the Scriptures tend to err because they do not know the power of God, and those who know the power of God tend to err because they do not know the Scriptures. The Lord has called us to walk in truth by knowing the Scriptures and the power of God. There is presently a great blending of these emphases, or overemphases if that is the case, which presents the greatest hope for the church since the first century.

The conflict between those who devote themselves to the Scriptures without knowing the power, or those who devote themselves mostly to the power without knowing the Scriptures well, is the basic conflict in the church between the prophetic/evangelist types and the pastor/teacher types. Both have essential truth, and both sides will remain in essential error until the conflict is resolved.

God ordained that all of these ministries are required for the proper equipping of His church. The Scriptures make it clear that all of these ministries, along with the apostle, are given **"*until* we all attain to the unity of the faith, and of the knowledge of the Son of God, to a mature man, to the measure of the stature which belongs to the fulness of Christ" (Ephesians 4:13).** Is there a fellowship anywhere in the world that measures up to this? Then obviously all of these ministries are still needed.

The Lord is going to restore true apostolic Christianity to the earth. To do this He is going to have to restore true apostles to the church. We cannot expect this until the prophets and teachers learn to worship the Lord together just as they did at Antioch. When they did this the Lord released possibly the two greatest missionary apostles of all time—Paul and Barnabas. The war between these ministries must end, and it will. The churches and movements that end it first, will be the first to cross the barrier into the final phase of church history. When this happens all of the gifts and ministries in the church will rise to their appropriate place.

Is There Nothing New?

A tragic misunderstanding of people who seek to be biblical comes from Solomon's statement; **"That which has been is that which will be, and that which has been done is that which will be done. So, there is nothing new under the sun" (Ecclesiastes 1:9).** There are historic and general senses in which this statement is true, but taking it to an extreme, this mentality will lead to a profound deception. The "new creation" itself was instituted by God after this statement was made. In fact, who could even count the many inventions and new things created since then? Our daily life is probably filled with more new things and experiences than we can count.

To understand the book of Ecclesiastes we must understand that it is written from the position of being "under the sun," or from the earthly, human perspective. This is an important book in the canon of Scripture because it reveals perceptions that men have when they are not able to see from the heavenly perspective. For example, this book declares that men are just beasts with no eternal destiny (see Ecclesiastes 3:18-22). This is not true, but it shows the limit of our view when we can only see things "from under the sun."

When this wrong concept, that there is nothing new, is applied to worship, or to our faith, it imposes a stagnation that will quickly dry up the rivers of life that are supposed to be flowing through us. One reason that the living water is found in a river, and not a pond or lake, is because living water is flowing, going somewhere. It has been said that, "You can never step into the same river twice." Because a river flows, it is constantly changing both its own path and the landscape around it. The Lord used the metaphor of water for truth because truth, like water, must flow in order to stay pure. If it stops flowing it will stagnate very fast.

It was the mind set of sameness and rigidity in worship that the Lord rejected, saying, **"This people draw near with their words, and honor Me with their lip service, but they remove their hearts far from Me, and** *their reverence for Me consists of tradition learned by rote"* **(Isaiah 29:13).** His exhortation was to, **"Sing to the** LORD **a** *new* **song" (Isaiah 42:10** KJV**).** In other places the Lord promised to put "a new spirit within us" (see Ezekiel 11:19); to do a "new thing" (see Isaiah 43:19); to give us **"a new commandment" (John 13:34** KJV**),** to make us **"new creatures" (II Corinthians 5:17** KJV**);** He **"inaugurated a new and living way" (Hebrews 10:20).** When we are born again **"all things become new" (II Corinthians 5:17** KJV**);** and we are to walk in **"the newness of life" (Romans 6:4** KJV**).** Ultimately, the Lord is going to make **"all things new" (Revelation 21:5** KJV**).**

The overwhelming testimony of the Scriptures is that God does many new things. Those who wrongly understand the one statement, "There is nothing new under the sun," inevitably been have those who were the most prone to miss what God was presently doing.

As Jeremiah observed, **"His compassions ... are** *new* **every morning" (Lamentations 3:22-23** KJV**).** Just as He revealed His mercy in a new way daily when He walked the earth, He is constantly showing His mercy in new ways with each of us. A wife may love flowers, but if her husband brought home the same type of bouquet every day, she would soon get bored with it. Our God is the greatest Lover who knows how to keep the relationship with His bride fresh. When the church submits to the pressure to conform, or to measure God's order by uniformity, she has made a devastating error.

Satan's Cord of Three Strands

Satan also has a cord of three strands which is not easily broken. It is composed of the religious spirit, the control spirit, and the political spirit.

The religious spirit seeks to have us base our spirituality on the performance of religious duties rather than by seeking a relationship with our Redeemer.

The control spirit works with the religious spirit to impose compliance, even with biblical standards, but a compliance imposed by external pressure rather than by the Spirit through a change of heart.

The political spirit empowers the first two by having us focus our attention on what men think rather than what God thinks. Satan has effectively used this cord to bind almost every new movement to date. The movement which effectively resists these attacks will unquestionably have the greatest potential for fully crossing over into the Promised Land that has been given to us in Christ.

Every new movement in the church has suffered a massive assault from the "thought police," who try to rob the movement of its freshness, and the people of their liberty in Christ. This is one of Satan's most effective ways to divert men from the essence of the true faith, a living relationship with God.

In this way, true faith is replaced by mere ritual and formula that make men into automatons who seek simply to fit in. Soon men are not seeking to be conformed to the image of Christ as much as they are seeking to conform to the image of the leaders of the movement. Even the newest and freshest forms of worship are quickly turned into new traditions which stringently resist further innovation or change. This will continue until we fully comprehend that our God is the Creator who will always be ultimately and profoundly creative. When we are truly joined to Him we will be like Him.

God does not change, and His nature has never changed. When He created man in His image one of the most basic characteristics of that image was creativity. When we have been fully delivered from the yoke of bondage, creativity will abound in us like never before. When the church is fully freed from the yoke of Satan's cord of three strands, she will become the very center of creativity, and science, on the earth. *True* science will always lead to the Creator. *True* art will always reveal Christ, through whom and for whom all things were made, and in whom all things will be consummated.

When the church enters into true worship, she will produce the greatest scientists and the greatest artists that the world has ever seen. The Lord knows all things. The gift of a word of knowledge is simply a brief touch of the mind of Christ who knows all things. When we are fully joined to the mind of Christ we will be getting much more than people's names and addresses! This may be a beginning, but we must go on from here. As we are joined to Him, having His mind, the very secrets of the universe will be opened to us—past, present, and future.

Resisting Religious Socialism

Socialism is dying or is in retreat almost everywhere, except in the church! Socialism was one of the ultimate manifestations of Satan's cord of three strands. It sought to shape everyone into the same mold. This excludes creative, individual character of man which is essential to the image of God in man that is to be recovered by redemption. Socialism essentially makes the institution the source, which removes both initiative and responsibility from men; this destroys creativity, a basic part of the nature of our Lord, who is the blessed Creator.

As the socialistic governments collapse, there will be a strong tendency for the church to try to take their place in providing many social needs. This is a deadly trap! The church is not the source, but is here to point men to the Source—Jesus. Jesus Christ really is the answer to every human problem, and can supply every human need. However, if the church tries to be the Holy Spirit to people, the very power of her gospel message will be diluted accordingly.

The church does have a place as a vessel through which the Lord can reach to touch the needs of His people. However, we must be very careful not to take the people's yokes, but to only do that which the Lord is leading us to do. Only then will He do the works through us. Without Him we will fail just as tragically as the socialist governments. The Lord could wave His hand and meet the needs of the whole world for all time, but He is obviously not doing this for a reason. Sometimes, not doing what we have not been called to do is harder than doing what we have been called to do. True obedience, and true worship, require this resolve.

Living in the *NEW* Creation

"New" is a word greatly feared by the rigid and insecure. However, those who talk the most about God doing a new thing are often those who are the most resistant to change. This tendency is called by psychologists "presenting a bold exterior in order to hide corruption on the inside." This explains why those who become the most vehement attackers of others are almost always found to be hiding serious sins of their own. Those who are the most rigid sticklers for doctrinal purity are often those who are the most prone to serious license with the Scriptures. This is why Paul told Timothy to **"pay close attention to yourself and to your teaching" (I Timothy 4:16).**

If you want to know what God is saying to almost any preacher, listen to his preaching. It has been the nature of the church to preach many things that we need to hear first and foremost. Possibly the most radical new thing that the world could ever witness would be a church that actually lives what it preaches. The new thing that God is trying to do in us is not a new truth, but a fresh revelation of the age old gospel, a revelation so real that we will really live by it. We must have fresh manna daily if we are going to make it to our promised land. That Manna is Jesus Christ.

As we discussed earlier, when the author of Hebrews exhorted us to leave **"the elementary teaching about the Christ" (Hebrews 6:1),** he did not mean that we should leave the teachings about Christ, but rather the *elementary* teachings about Him. We must go on to the deeper revelations of Christ.

The book of Hebrews is considered the deepest and most profound of the New Testament, but the author rebuked his readers because they should have been eating meat but he could only give them what he considered "milk" for spiritual babies (see Hebrews 5:12-14). How are we ever going to eat meat if we cannot even digest what the New Testament considers milk? Yet that same New Testament book exhorts us to leave the elementary teachings and go on.

Jesus is no longer a carpenter from Nazareth. He is a King beyond our comprehension of what a king is. He dwells in glory beyond any earthly comprehension of glory. The riches of His wisdom extend beyond our limited ability to comprehend. We are impressed when we supernaturally receive someone's name or physical affliction by a word of knowledge, and we should be, because this is wonderful. Even so, we must understand that there is much more available. We are just scratching the surface of His heavenly knowledge!

The Lord upholds the universe by the word of His power. He has unlimited knowledge of each person on earth, and if we become of one mind with Him, the supernatural knowledge that we have access to will greatly transcend what we are touching now. Let us not despise the small beginnings, but let us also understand that we are far from walking in all that God has made available to us by His Holy Spirit.

The power of the One who created all things lives within everyone of us! We are supposed to be seated with Him in the heavenly places (see Ephesians 2:6). What would the world really look like from that perspective? Before the end there will be a people who will find out.

We are now coming to the time when new moves of God will be arising at a pace we have never before witnessed. This is going to happen because men are going to break the shackles placed upon Christianity. They will have little regard for what religious men might think of them, or say about them. New congregations will be springing up almost everywhere, who really have fresh manna. If we do not have it they will take all of our people, because the people are going to go to where the presence of the Lord is, and where He is setting the table.

God is about to make a frontal assault on the delusion of His church that has kept her captive to the pressures of conformity and uniformity. He really is going to renew our minds. Those who experience His mercy in a new way every morning will be made new every morning, and they will begin to bring continual new birth to the world. They will have such security in their relationship with Him that they will be able to embrace the new things that He is doing without the present paranoia that so dominates the church.

This will be a most unsettling time for those who are bound by Satan's cord of three strands. To the rest it will be like the coming of the bluest sky after the longest of storms. The very definition that men have given to Christianity will change over the next few years. The world will not be able to put what is ahead into its neat little categories for religion.

The world is about to be filled with marvel and wonder at what it sees and hears coming from the church. This will interest the world to the point that church news will become a constant part of the national and international news. When true worship is released in the church, our meetings will become more interesting than sports or concerts of the now popular "idols."

True worship touches the heart of man like nothing else can because it touches the heart of God. We were created for His pleasure, and there is nothing more fulfilling for the human soul than fulfilling this purpose. As the church becomes what she was created to be, the world will witness the most secure, fulfilled and creative people it has ever seen.

Even though there will be so many new movements arising, they will flow together in a harmony that no power of man could have controlled. The church will become the greatest revelation of the symphony of God's great diversity, and she will capture the attention and imagination of the entire world.

The Boast of Satan

Early in Israel's journey from Egypt, the people fell into such debauchery that the Lord threatened to destroy them all except Moses. Moses interceded for the people by declaring that if the Lord destroyed them the whole world would believe that God had the power to deliver the people out of Egypt, but He did not have the power to bring them into the Promised Land. God listened to Moses and patiently waited for that generation to pass away, and then led the next generation into the Promised Land.

Today Satan boasts that even though God can redeem men, He cannot change them. Before the end comes, God will have the witness of a church on the earth that is not only redeemed, but changed. His church will not continue to reflect the evils of the world, but will be changed into the image of His Son. Before the end there will be a church without spot or wrinkle. That it is without spot speaks of her purity. That it is without wrinkle speaks of her perpetual youthfulness. The bride will have made herself ready for the bridegroom, and the world and devils will no longer have the boast that the church is no different from them.

Born for Greatness

A common characteristic by which men or events are judged "great" is their uniqueness. Uniqueness does not necessarily make one great, but no one has been considered great who was not unique. It is the ability to go beyond the limits, to break the yoke of the status quo, that is essential for any who would attain greatness. It was by Abraham's willingness to leave his home and family in the greatest culture on earth, that enabled him to become one of the greatest men of all time. Abraham is the father of faith, and such is the nature of all who walk by the true faith. He went out "not knowing where he was going," but he did know what he was looking for—he was looking for what God was building, not men.

When Jesus was confronted by the Pharisees who claimed to be "the sons of Abraham," He replied, **"If you are Abraham's children, do the deeds of Abraham" (John 8:39).** If we are the true sons of Abraham we, too, will do the deeds that he did. The present world, with all of its genius, culture, science or wealth, will not be as compelling to us as wandering in a wilderness seeking what God is doing.

Those who walk by faith seldom know where they are going, but they do know exactly what they are looking for—the city which God is building. For those who have this vision there is nothing in this life that is not worth sacrificing to walk in His purposes. We are called not only to seek what He is building, but to become a part of that building. This is the ultimate quest of man, and no man will find true satisfaction in anything else.

The church of the last days is called to greatness. We will find our greatness when we become free enough to pursue this ultimate quest. We would be hard pressed to point to any church today that was not built by men in order to attract men. There is a generation that will arise that will not build in order to attract men, but to attract God. That will be the most radical devotion to have been witnessed on earth for nearly twenty centuries. The early church turned the world upside down with its message. The last day church will turn an upside down world right side up.

The spiritual generation arising will be true sons of Abraham. They will cross the barrier that the previous generations would not cross, and they will possess the Promised Land. A great demarcation is now taking place in the church. We will either be a part of the generation that perishes in the wilderness, or the one that crosses over. Having the faith to be different will be one of the distinguishing characteristics of those who overcome.

CHAPTER NINETEEN

Catching the Wave

There is a great spiritual advance that is now gaining momentum throughout the body of Christ. It has the potential to be as sweeping in its scope and impact as the greatest movements of church history. How can we discern it accurately, and position ourselves properly to be a part of it?

Moves of the Holy Spirit are often compared to waves because their characteristics are common. There is a difference between catching the waves of the Holy Spirit and being blown about by every new wind of doctrine. If the Holy Spirit moves in waves, how do we catch them so as to be carried in the direction that He is going?

There are four basic steps that a surfer uses that can give us significant insight into what we, too, must do to catch the waves of the Holy Spirit. If a surfer is going to catch a wave he must first discern where it is going to break. Second, he must position himself properly at that point. Third, he must begin to move in the direction that the wave is going. Then he must not hesitate when it breaks, or it will just pass him by.

Looking Back to Look Ahead

Many are discerning enough to know that the Holy Spirit is moving again, but are doing very little to position themselves properly to be a part of it. Every move of God is built upon the foundation of the previous moves. If we are going to discern where the next move of God is going to break, we need to discern the nature and pattern of the previous ones.

James gave an interesting exhortation concerning treatment of the Law, which was the "movement" that preceded Christianity:

Do not speak against one another, brethren. He who speaks against a brother, or judges his brother, speaks against the law, and judges the law; but if you judge the law, you are not a doer of the law, but a judge of it.

There is only one Lawgiver and Judge, the One who is able to save and to destroy; but who are you who judge your neighbor?

Do not complain, brethren, against one another, that you yourselves may not be judged; behold, the Judge is standing right at the door (James 4:11-12; 5:9).

When we judge out of a critical spirit, we are condemning ourselves to the opposition of God, Who **"resists the proud, but gives grace to the humble" (James 4:6).** To become proud of our own standing is to depart from the very foundation upon which we are standing—God's grace. However, there is a "righteous judgment" that we must have.

We are foolish if we do not try to learn from the mistakes of the previous movements. Even so, we must be careful how we view them, not as condemning our spiritual parents, but seeing where the potential for the same faults exists within us so that we can seek the grace to stand in those areas.

The failure to properly understand righteous and unrighteous judgment is the reason for many of the greatest failures of the church in history, and is one of the most important issues facing the church today. Until we understand them, and walk by that understanding, we will continue to stumble over a deadly stumbling block.

The church, both historically and currently, has been prone to use unrighteous judgment while neglecting the righteous judgment. Many watchdog ministries and Christian journalists have stumbled into the yoke of the accuser while sincerely trying to help fill a tragic void in church government. They fall because they have moved into a realm of authority to which they have not been appointed. Meanwhile, the elders neglect the authority which they have been given to exercise. Every new movement will continue to fall short of its potential until this important issue is resolved.

We must be able to properly analyze our mistakes, and bring the needed correction, or we will continue to stumble over the same stumbling blocks. However, self-appointed watchmen will not be able to do this without letting more of the enemy in than they are able to keep out. The elders of the church must stand up to take their proper place to fill this void, or we will continue to have this confusion.

Paddling with the Wave

Some are both discerning where the next wave is going to break, and are positioning themselves properly, but are hesitant to move forward until the wave is upon them. These are in as much danger of missing the wave as those who have not positioned themselves at all. The most important thing that we can do to be moving with the wave when it comes is to obey and implement that which was imparted to the church through the last move.

Many of these last waves which have already crashed on the shore and retreated, brought something of value with them which the church desperately needs if we are going to be fully prepared for our last day mandate. The reason that the accuser has so ruthlessly attacked the remnants of these movements is because he knows very well that they contained something of great significance that the church needs.

It is true that these movements may have made many great mistakes, and that significant doctrinal errors crept into most of them, but this was all intended to divert them from the important message that they carried. We are now in desperate need of the truths that they carried, and we need elders with enough confidence in the Holy Spirit to lead them into all truth to examine the wreckage of these movements for this treasure.

Many hesitate and miss the moves of the Holy Spirit because of a religious spirit rooted in human idealism that will not move until something is "totally God." The Lord does not do anything without man, and Jesus was the only man who ever walked on this earth who did everything in total obedience to God. Those who are under the delusion that something must be totally God before they will become a part of it are almost totally sure to miss God.

I heard a story about a farmer who was once being congratulated by a minister on the precision and lushness of his cornfield, remarking that he could not have done that without God. "I agree," said the farmer, "But He could not do it without me either. You should see the field I let Him grow by Himself. It's all weeds!"

There is an important point to this story. God commissioned man to "cultivate the garden." Man's work on earth is not unnatural, but man is a part of the nature of the world which God created. Likewise, He has commissioned fallible men to do the work of the ministry. Even the greatest man of God is an earthen vessel, imperfect and frail. James explained that, **"We all stumble in many ways" (James 3:2 NIV).**

The Lord left the church in the hands of men who appeared to be quite unstable and prone to mistakes, and they did make mistakes. We all must grow in grace and wisdom. If we had to wait until we were perfect to minister, no one would ever be qualified. Perfectionists who set unrealistic standards are like the Pharisees who would not enter the kingdom themselves, and tried to hinder everyone else from entering as well.

Every true move of God has begun with a considerable amount of humanity mixed in at first. There will always be tares mixed in with the wheat. If we wait until all of the tares are removed, we will miss the entire harvest.

Wait for the Big One

If we want to catch the biggest wave, we must resist catching the smaller ones. There are patterns to incoming waves which experienced surfers learn to recognize. Patience is required if they are going to ride the biggest and best wave. Likewise, in the Spirit there are many movements to which we can give ourselves, and many projects we can become involved in, but are they what we have been called to? How many of these are only working to displace us from our position when the big one comes?

This should not discourage anyone from devotion to service and ministry. Indeed, the only way that we will be in shape and skilled enough to catch the big wave is by practicing on the smaller ones. However, when we have been adequately prepared, and we know that the big one is coming, we must let the smaller ones go by. Many who miss the great moves of God do so because they are already too busy.

The Opposition

Each wave will try to make it as far up the beach as it can. Then the wave recedes, undercutting the next wave, making it break sooner than it would otherwise. Seldom have those who were a part of one move of God gone on to be a part of the next move. Usually those of a previous move are retreating as the next wave advances, creating a clash that hinders its progress. Some of the greatest opposition of every incoming wave will be from the previous waves that are retreating.

This has been true throughout church history. However, even though this has continually been our history, it does not have to be our future. Before the end there will be a movement that will capture the hearts of those in the previous movements so that they will join the advance rather than continue to retreat. This will happen when the hearts of the fathers have been turned to the children. When this happens the church will begin a spiritual advance that will prevail until the end of the age.

Looking at some of the historic factors that have caused others to retreat can help us discern these stumbling blocks. The first dangerous delusion is for us to think that we would never oppose a true move of God. It has happened to some of the greatest men of God in history. Andrew Murray is a good example of how even a great man of God, with a passion for seeing revival come to the church, can fail to recognize the very revival for which he had spent his entire life praying.

The cause for this tragic failure was the fact that the revival that he hoped for, and even prophesied of, did not come in the form that he was expecting. Though he earnestly desired to see the release of spiritual gifts within the church again, he was offended by the package they arrived in.

Unfortunately, most new movements are led by relatively immature leaders. This is because the mature leaders have become "old wineskins," too inflexible to receive the new wine. Spiritual movements must be led by the Spirit, Who requires flexibility and openness. Usually the only ones He can find that are flexible enough are the immature, because they have not yet become inflexible with preconceived ideas.

Immature leaders are therefore more prone to be dependent on the Holy Spirit than their experience, allowing Him to direct as He chooses. This is probably why the Lord chose such unlikely and "unqualified" men as the foundational leaders of His church. They were so unqualified that they were desperately dependent upon His grace and guidance.

A Higher Way

Rarely does there arise a spiritual leader with great experience and wisdom, combined with a sensitive dependency upon the Holy Spirit. However, such leadership is certainly preferable to that of the immature. The immature do allow the Holy Spirit to lead, which is the highest form of wisdom, but they often allow other influences to gain entry because of their lack of experience. To counter this, the Lord always seems to give opportunity to leaders of previous movements to lead the next move. The greatest leaders will know how to let the Holy Spirit lead, while having the experience and discernment to keep the movement out of the hands of the lawless or legalistic.

Two good biblical examples of those with maturity and experience combined with flexibility and dependency on the Holy Spirit are Joshua and Caleb. Such will also be required for the movement that leads the church across her Jordan River into the battle for her Promised Land. Not only were Joshua and Caleb men of great faith in the Lord, but their faith was not diluted by many years of wandering in the wilderness with a faithless people.

Such faith could only be the result of two great spiritual factors. First, true faith is not encouraged or discouraged by the condition of the people, because it is not faith in people but in God. Second, true faith is not limited by time but always views from the perspective of eternity. That is why the great men of faith in Scripture were content to view the fulfillment of the promises prophetically without having to receive them in their own time.

It is most difficult to grow in wisdom, experience and age compared to other men while remaining humble. This is because of our tendency to judge ourselves by our comparison to other men, rather than to the only true Standard—Christ Jesus. Measuring ourselves by other men, or our church by other churches, is one of the most deadly stumbling blocks to spiritual leaders. Paul identified this error; **"but when they measure themselves by themselves, and compare themselves with themselves, they are without understanding" (II Corinthians 10:12).**

Those who possess true faith do not look at men, nor at the temporal; they are not short-sighted. The truly wise will not be overly encouraged when men gather around them, or discouraged when they depart. If we receive our encouragement from men it only proves that we have received our authority from men. If we receive our authority from above, then no man can take it away, and we will not be overly concerned by either the approval or disapproval of men.

How many of us could, like Philip, begin a revival that stirs an entire city, then give that work into the hands of others so that we can go witness to just one man? The reason that Philip could be entrusted with such authority and power to stir a city was because of his obedience. If he were just focused on men, or the temporary, he would never have left Samaria.

It is probable that the fruit of that one Ethiopian eunuch's conversion was much greater than the revival in Samaria. Centuries later, missionaries were astonished to find that when they arrived in Ethiopia there were so many Christians already there. This fruit had been hidden to men, and probably even to Philip, but it was certainly credited to his account.

Obedience, Not Sacrifice

It is obedience, not sacrifice, that will keep us in the will of God. I do not think that I have ever met a true Christian that did not long to be in the center of the activity of God. However, we must know that not all good activity is God's activity. We must also understand that it is not possible for all of us to be a part of everything that He is doing. The most important issue is not just catching the "big wave," but catching the one that He wants us to catch, while cheering on those who may be catching the bigger ones, and the smaller ones, if they are in God's will.

As we keep our vision on the goal of seeing the water move as far up the beach as possible, and holding all of the ground that we can take, we will be in a better position to move forward with the next wave rather than retreating and undercutting it. It does not matter who leads a wave as long as The Leader gets the glory. To have any other attitude would be ludicrous, as though the donkey's colt, on which Jesus rode into Jerusalem, thought that all of the commotion and adoration was for him instead of the One riding on his back.

One of the great leadership lessons in nature is found with migrating waterfowl such as geese and ducks. They fly in "V" formations because the lead bird creates a draft that makes the flying easier for those who follow closely behind him. However, since the lead bird cutting through the air is doing the most work, he will only stay on the point for a period of time, and then he will drop back to the end of the formation and rest. This rotation allows the birds to share the burden of leadership, and all benefit from the draft when others are leading. If a bird refused to give up his leadership position at the proper time he would begin to slow down the whole flock. Those who give up their position at the proper time will have a chance to rest while following in the wake of others, enabling them to again assume the point at another time.

Seldom in church history has any leader been on the cutting edge for more than a few years. However, it is a most difficult thing for a leader to give up leadership. For those who refused, there was a clear demarcation in their lives, marking the point at which they stopped going forward and started attacking those who did.

Flying geese do not have as their goal to be the point bird, but rather to get to their destination. Whenever our own position becomes a goal in itself we will become more of a hindrance to the advancement of the church than a leader of it. Unfortunately, a man can have great influence and control other people long after he has lost the true anointing for spiritual leadership. King Saul is one of the more obvious biblical examples of this principle.

Saul's counterpart, King David, was an extraordinary leader in his own time, but he had the wisdom to realize the limits of his authority. When he understood that it was not his destiny to build the temple, he began gathering materials to pass on to his heir in order to make his job easier. The greatest leaders not only know how far to go themselves—they know how to prepare for the next generation, and when to pass the scepter.

Summary

Leadership is a valuable gift. The desire to be on the cutting edge of what God is doing, to be in the center of the action, is often evidence that one really loves the Lord and wants to be a part of what He is doing. It can also be one of the most prideful, and disobedient desires we can have, if our motives are not right.

It is right to want to push back the darkness, to help the body of Christ climb to higher ground, but are we doing this for the Lord's glory or for our own? If we are not doing it for ourselves we should be just as glad to prepare for others to do it, and to cheer them on. Is that not what the great cloud of witnesses is doing right now for us?

Being on the cutting edge, or being with a group that is, is not the most important thing in life. When we stand before the throne of God on that great judgment day, He is not going to count how many cutting edge movements we were a part of. We are going to be judged on our obedience, and how much of His likeness we bear. In Christ it is true that the greatest leaders are the greatest followers. The more closely we follow Him, the more of His glory we will behold, and the more like Him we will become. That is the essence of true ministry—to be so close to Him that we become like, that we might reveal Him.

This is the first volume in a series devoted to the practical equipping of the saints in the biblical gifts and ministries.